AI Leadership Compass

Lead with Clarity: 7 Moves That Power AI Transformation

By Priya Sarathy PhD

Logos Ethos Pathos Publishing
Pittsburgh, Pennsylvania

Copyright

Advance Praise

As someone who is navigating the complexities of AI development & usage on a day-to-day basis, *"AI Leadership Compass"* is a timely guide to navigating AI adoption with strategic clarity. Priya Sarathy's emphasis on *human-in-the-loop* oversight is crucial, particularly in an era of rapid automation. Her discussion of GM's predictive AI for supply chain risk management highlights how intentional data curation drives business value. For leaders seeking to scale AI responsibly, this book offers frameworks and foresight needed to turn potential into performance.

- Raghu Kulkarni, Chief AI officer, Equifax

AI holds tremendous opportunity for transforming organizations, our culture, and global economies. But transformation for the sake of Fear of Missing Out (FOMO) is not the right strategy. Strategic value should drive decision about what and where AI should be applied and/or installed. The AI Leadership Compass provides a practical framework for evaluating use cases and assigning value to them. The case studies and use cases make it real. And the Executive Reflections offer a **guided opportunity to think about your use case** and apply a value framework. This was exactly the message I needed to read right now as we are all finding our way forward in the Intelligence Age of AI.

- Morgan Templar, CEO, First CDO Partners

Want to do more with AI but feeling stuck? Then this book is for you - it demystifies AI and **inspires and empowers leaders for actionable AI**. Through illustrative case studies drawn from various industries, executive reflections, and simple frameworks to guide the readers, the author offers a clear-eyed roadmap to derive strategic value from AI. If your organization is investing in AI, read the book to know what questions you should ask to ensure AI success.

- Anandhi Bharadwaj, Goizueta Endowed Chair in Electronic Commerce and Professor of Information Systems & Operations Management, Emory University

In today's rapidly evolving landscape of data and AI, it is crucial for leaders to effectively utilize resources like these to generate significant value. This book offers a clear and concise AI strategy, guiding leaders through every step—from developing a robust data strategy and fostering AI fluency and literacy within their organizations, to measuring the tangible impact and value of AI initiatives, and ultimately, building a fully AI-enabled enterprise with Responsible AI safeguards. As the book illustrates, it empowers AI leaders to **become skilled orchestrators of AI value realization.**

-   Faizan Javed, Sr. Director Data Science and Engineering, Kaiser Permanente

Dr. Priya Sarathy's AI Leadership Compass is the kind of book every business leader should read if they want to make AI a core competency for their company. She takes a complicated topic and breaks it down into manageable, engaging chapters filled with examples from everyday life and practical use cases.

What stood out to me was how each section ends with reflection prompts and actions to take making it easier to connect the dots between the ideas and your company's AI goals. This guide deepened my understanding of how AI can enhance organizational performance by enabling smarter, faster, and more consistent decision-making.

> -   *Alka Citrin, Scheller College of Business,*
> *Georgia Tech*

Dedication

To my father and my father-in-law—
who embraced not only logic and reason,
but viewed life rooted in curiosity, compassion, and the dignity of
human differences.

Table of Contents

AI Leadership Compass

Lead with Clarity: 7 Moves That Power AI Transformation

Foreword

I had the pleasure of working with Priya Sarathy at Equifax. Priya joined our fraud data and analytics team where she was able to drive product innovation and development at-scale. What impressed me was her ability to drive strategic design with execution among diverse cross functional delivery teams. Her passion and leadership for combining strategy with delivery was infectious. That same clarity, pragmatism and vision runs through every page of this book.

AI Leadership Compass is not another abstract or overly technical exploration of artificial intelligence. It is a practical, accessible, and strategic guidebook for leaders and organizations seeking to safely and collectively embed AI into their business. Priya introduces a set of leadership and management practices that are grounded in real-world experience and informed by the challenges that many companies are facing as they move from AI experimentation to operationalization.

What makes this book stand out is its insistence on application. The reflection questions at the end of each chapter do not let you skim the surface. They challenge you to go deeper with your teams, to ask what these frameworks mean for your organization, and to surface conversations that matter. AI adoption is not just about technology— it is about behavior change, readiness, and accountability. This book understands that deeply.

There are several insights I found especially helpful.

First, Priya shows how existing data management and governance practices can be extended into AI. This does two important things: First, it makes it less daunting for those organizations looking to scale AI management, and it grounds the work in familiar territory. She provides examples that are drawn from actual organizations—proof that the shift to AI is not about starting over but about evolving what you already do well.

Second, she tackles a topic that few address directly: Specifically, how organizations need to be ready for the overwhelm of data that AI organizations will create. Many organizations are improving their data quality to generate high quality AI models —but Priya goes further. She reminds us that the data generated by AI itself must also be managed, governed, and held to quality standards.

This is not a trivial topic, and it is impressive that she tackles it here. Readers of her book will know and can plan for the need to manage and improve the data quality of the data created by AI. This book pushes readers to build the discipline—and the fortitude—to focus on reproducibility, value realization, and long-term scale.

AI Leadership Compass is a playbook for those who want to lead AI with strategy, with clarity, and with their teams—not ahead of them. It doesn't promise easy answers, but it gives you the questions and strategic frameworks to make better decisions and how to scale the value of AI holistically and collectively from the beginning. And in this fast-moving space, that's exactly what leaders need most.

If you are considering how to begin applying and embedding data discipline and AI in your organization— not just using it, but leading with it— this is a fast paced and highly accessible book

Peter Maynard
Chief Data and Analytics Officer
Guardian Life

Introduction

Navigating Intelligence with Intent

AI is no longer reserved for R&D labs or tech giants. It now shapes everyday tools, customer experiences, and enterprise workflows. Yet for many business leaders, AI still feels elusive and powerful. At the same time there is a perception that it is opaque and difficult to manage. Too often, organizations pursue AI initiatives without clear goals, foundational readiness, or the strategic leadership needed to convert potential into performance.

This book was written to change that.

AI Leadership Compass is designed to help business decision-makers navigate the complexity of AI adoption with confidence and clarity. It draws on years of hands-on experience helping organizations define data strategies, develop governance frameworks, build AI capabilities, and, most importantly, align them to real business value.

The leaders I work with do not need another technical deep dive. They need tools for thinking, frameworks for alignment, and a shared language to guide teams through uncertainty. They need to understand not just what AI can do, but how to decide what it *should* do and why.

Over the years, I have led analytics teams by steadily cultivating a data-driven culture by building awareness of both its potential and its pitfalls across legal, product, and technology functions. One lesson stands out: without a community of AI-aware and AI-fluent leaders, even the most well-intentioned guidance often slips through the cracks.

To streamline build, enable, and deliver AI projects in a successful manner, we need to "train the trainer", that is our AI leadership teams. Whether you're just getting started or navigating the next wave of scale, this guide gives you the tools to think strategically, act intentionally, and lead with clarity.

This book is written in a conversational, tactical style, designed to give you just enough grounding to begin your deeper exploration of:

- Strategic frameworks that connect AI design to business outcomes

- Use cases that reflect real-world complexity, not idealized pilot projects

- Reflective prompts to help you evaluate your organization's readiness

- Lessons from failures and insights from leaders who've scaled AI responsibly

The chapters follow the lifecycle of AI readiness: beginning with foundational data strategy, progressing through governance, training, and capability building, and concluding with enterprise enablement and measurement. You do not need to read it cover-to-cover to benefit. Each chapter can serve as a guidepost, wherever you are in your AI journey.

This leadership journey is grounded in seven key moves. Practical behaviours and mindset shift that help organizations lead with clarity, not chaos. Each move is anchored to one or more of three essential leadership levers: **Strategic Vision, Culture & Capability, and Delivery & Governance**. These are not standalone actions; they complement and reinforce one another as the foundation for responsible and impactful AI leadership. Multiple chapters discuss and illustrate the dimensions of each move.

These moves are how modern leaders guide AI adoption. Not through command-and-control, but through alignment, adaptability, and shared understanding. The chapters address each of these moves as connected narratives. At the end of each chapter, we reference the key move as a specific takeaway to help build better understanding of the moves.

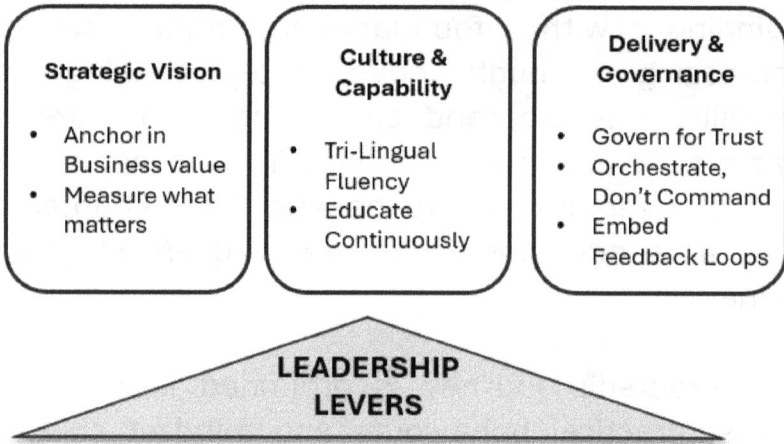

Strategic Vision	Culture & Capability	Delivery & Governance
• Anchor in Business value • Measure what matters	• Tri-Lingual Fluency • Educate Continuously	• Govern for Trust • Orchestrate, Don't Command • Embed Feedback Loops

LEADERSHIP LEVERS

Figure 1: AI Leadership moves that matter

Analogies and case studies are provided to link the moves to real applications. These are just to get you started on recognizing the solutions AI are driving. Explore some of the keywords to discover additional use cases.

If you are a leader navigating AI for the first time, this book is your compass.

If you are scaling from early pilots to enterprise-wide transformation, this is your map.

If you are somewhere in between balancing risk, pressure, and opportunity, this book offers direction, clarity, and reassurance.

You do not have to lead with all the answers- just the right questions, the right mindset, and the intention to lead with purpose.

Let's get started.

— Priya Sarathy

Use this compass to trace how each of the 7 Moves shows up across the chapters—and the leadership decisions they influence.

Leadership Move	Chapters Aligned	Description
Anchor in Business Value	Ch. 1, Ch. 5, Ch. 9, Ch. 13	Aligning AI with strategic goals, data value, and enterprise capability.
Tri-Lingual Fluency	Ch. 7, Ch. 15	Promote fluency across data, tech, and domain to improve collaboration.
Measure What Matters	Ch. 5, Ch. 16	Emphasize outcome-based metrics linking AI to business value.
Govern for Trust, Not Control	Ch. 3, Ch. 4, Ch. 14	Govern AI inputs/outputs, risk, and responsible design.
Orchestrate, Do not Command	Ch. 6, Ch. 10, Ch. 15	Encourage coordination, human oversight, and distributed innovation.
Educate Continuously	Ch. 7, Ch. 8, Ch. 12	Build role-based fluency and risk-aware AI training at scale.
Embed Feedback Loops	Ch. 2, Ch. 6, Ch. 11	Support iterative learning, platform observability, and continuous improvement.

Figure 2: Mapping the 7 AI Leadership Moves Across the Book

Chapter 1: The Strategic Value of Data for AI

"AI is only as good as the data that fuels it."

In the past decade, artificial intelligence has moved from the lab to the boardroom. But while technology has evolved rapidly, the real bottleneck to AI success in business is not model complexity or computing power. It is data. For business leaders, the critical insight is this:

> *"Data is not just the input to AI. It is the foundation of your organization's ability to realize AI-driven value."*

As mundane as it sounds, all businesses do realize that data is their secret formulae. Coca-Cola famously stored its secret formula in a secure vault at SunTrust Bank (now Truist) in Atlanta. This is a testament to the value placed on proprietary data even before the digital age. Similarly, in 1873, German immigrants Adolph Coors and Jacob Schueler purchased a Pilsner-style beer recipe and launched a brewery that would eventually be valued at $17.8 billion. These are examples of how unstructured data recipes, processes, and know-how have held strategic value long before the AI era.

Figure 3: Timeline Captured through Unstructured Data

The Coca Cola historical timeline shown above communicates rich data about the branding, look and size of the product.

Fast forward to 2022: The launch of ChatGPT

Generative Pre-Trained Models (GPT models) ushered in an era of widespread awareness around large language models (LLMs), transformers, and AI agents. In just two years, the AI landscape has evolved dramatically with billions invested in data collection and model training. While the strategic value of data is well recognized, the question remains: How do you recognize structure and extract the value of your organization's data effectively for AI initiatives?

The Big Problem

Despite significant investments in AI, over 80% of AI projects fail to scale or deliver measurable ROI. Why? Because data feeding these systems are either unavailable, unstructured, untrusted, or not aligned to business objectives. Leaders are often unaware of the strategic work required to make data ready for AI. For decades, businesses have collected and safeguarded data and yet those same protections have often made data difficult to explore, share, or use for innovation. While compliance mandates have driven careful control, the lack of mature governance frameworks has created overly conservative environments where the true strategic potential of data is rarely realized.

Strategic Insight: What is Strategic Data?

Strategic data is:

- **Fit for Purpose**: Relevant to a specific business goal or AI use case
- **Trusted:** High-quality, governed, and traceable
- **Available:** Accessible in the right format, at the right time
- **Valuable**: Linked to measurable business outcomes

Thinking of data strategically requires a shift from "collect everything" to "curate the right things."

In the supply chain sector, distribution channels are important conduits that ensure the delivery of packages happens in a timely manner. Does this mean that a logistics organization, like UPS, is collecting data from all distribution channels and solving a global logistics problem ALL the time? No, they also must run a sustainable business. But distribution channels are the key purpose of the business. UPS does focus on the destinations of its packages to understand the distribution routes. They collect information specific to those routes and consider alternate routes that may be back-up options for these key delivery routes.

The need to focus on purpose is critical, not only for standard operations, but especially when applied to AI-led use cases. When data is grounded in clear business use cases, it forms a strategic bridge to the organization's goals. In later chapters, we'll explore what makes data trusted, valuable, and ready for AI-driven work.

Think about why you insure your home. The house provides comfort, security, and long-term value of invested assets. To protect it against the risk of disaster, insurance is your disaster recovery plan. Avoiding disaster comes second. To preserve and protect what we've already built, we invest in security systems, strong doors, and quality materials. Established organizations focus on business continuity as the first step before aiming for growth.

The same logic applies to data. To realize the long-term benefits of your AI and analytics investments, you must build with continuity in mind and safeguard against known and unknown risks. That means investing in high-quality data sources, applying governance practices early, and establishing recovery and backup plans. These are not just IT tasks, they're strategic imperatives.

Maintaining the value of your current data assets through proper treatment becomes a foundation for strategic vision. Restores, recovery, and redundancy plans must be part of your business continuity blueprint, especially as AI initiatives introduce new dependencies across systems, processes, and teams.

Data as a Strategic Asset

In AI, the value of data compounds with use. Once data is structured, cleaned, and labeled, it can:

- Power multiple AI use cases
- Be reused and enriched across the enterprise
- Become the basis for new data products or services
- Inform strategic decisions with greater speed and confidence

Connecting the strategic ability of data that 'keeps giving' and delivering ROI against business goals merits handling it as a strategic asset.

Use Case

Manufacturing:
Predictive Maintenance (PdM) in Manufacturing

In global manufacturing firms have invested in AI to reduce machine downtime. Initially, they struggled with inconsistent sensor data and missing maintenance records. By strategically aligning data collection to the predictive maintenance use case, they:

- Standardized IoT sensor data formats
- Digitized maintenance logs
- Mapped failure codes to machine types

Additional use cases can be found to explain the impact on reduced downtime from unanticipated failures and machinery breakdowns (IBM 2025).

The lesson: A significant reduction in unplanned outages and prevention of equipment repairs can be mitigated with strategic use of data and AI tools. Like the smoke detectors and burglar alarms in your home!

Because data is a strategic asset, organizations must pay close attention to how it is collected, stored, transformed, and used. Later chapters emphasize that ensuring data quality is essential to unlocking its full value

Executive Reflection

What does this discussion bring to the forefront of your mind? When do you reflect on the use of data in your organization and the AI efforts underway?

1. Do you know what data is feeding your AI efforts today?
2. Is your data aligned to the business outcomes that you care most about?
3. What barriers exist to making your data more trustworthy and accessible?

Call to Action: Map Strategic Data Priorities

List 2-3 key business goals. For each, answer:

- What data do we need to achieve this goal?
- Where is that data today? Who owns it?
- How well do we trust and understand this data?

This simple map becomes your strategic data opportunity canvas.

Summary

Data is not just fuel for AI; *it is the foundation for realizing value*. Not all data is an asset. This chapter explored why business-aligned, trusted, and purpose-driven data is essential for scaling AI. It challenged the assumption that *more data is always better* and instead introduced the idea of curating the right data to support strategic outcomes. The goal is to create such purpose-driven data assets.

Lessons Learned

- Strategic data is curated, trusted, and business-aligned; not just collected in volume.
- Historical and analog examples remind us that unstructured knowledge has long held enterprise value.
- Organizations must treat curated data like an asset to be managed, governed, and invested in, and with the intention of reuse.
- If data is not used, it delivers no return. Business value comes from business-goal driven data activation.

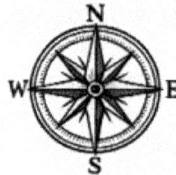

ANCHOR IN BUSINESS VALUE

Chapter 2: Designing a Data Supply Chain That Serves AI

"Data is the raw material; design your supply chain to refine, not just move it."

From Raw to Ready: The Role of the Data Supply Chain

AI systems can consume raw data. For focused AI applications to optimize value extraction, the systems rely on curated, contextual, and timely data feeds. Designing a data supply chain requires deliberate engineering of processes through which raw data is transformed into AI-ready data assets. A well-designed data supply chain ensures that raw data is transformed into decision-ready insights in a reliable, transparent, and scalable manner.

Consider how we spice up our lives with flavors of cloves and nutmeg. What makes a pumpkin pie aroma stir up memories? Nutmeg and cloves! The western world's historical exploration of these commodities launched global trade routes that were meticulously planned, managed, and defended. Control and governance of key ports and islands were central to trading advantage. Similarly, modern supply chains are sophisticated webs. For instance, General Motors sources components from over 200 Original Equipment

Manufacturers (OEM's). To succeed, they must understand the origins, quality, and assembly potential of every part. The same is true for data in AI ecosystems.

Success is only guaranteed if one is aware and literate about the parts that make up the sum: where they come from, the circumstances of each of the OEM manufacturers' environments, and tools and skills for the GM plant workers around the use and assembly of these parts. The sum of individual parts-quality should create equal or greater quality of the finished product.

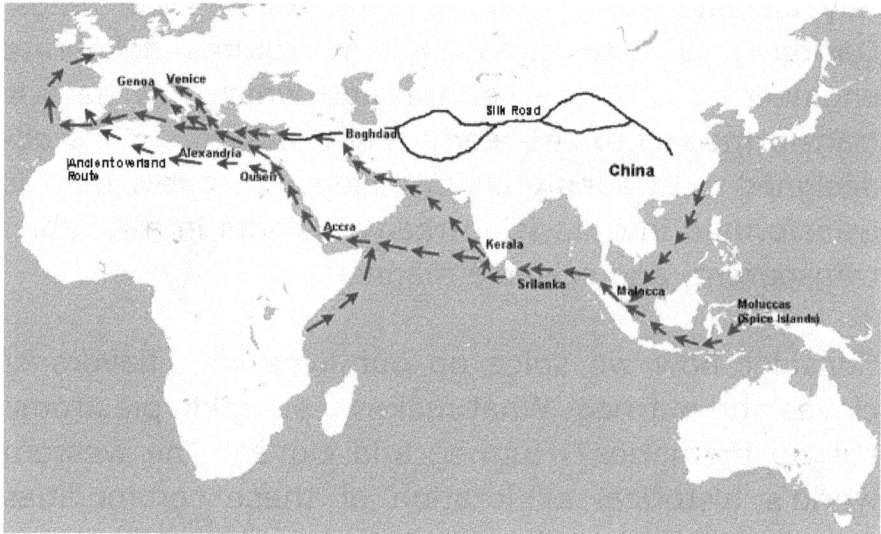

Figure 4: Spice Supply Chain-Value of Peppers and Cloves

"If AI is the engine, data is the fuel—and supply chain is the pipeline that delivers it."
- *Shared viewpoint*

Disruptions of the flow of data due to process, technology, or people can impact on the quality of data, its readiness to be used or its role as a strategic asset.

The Big Problem

Most organizations have fragmented data systems. Business leaders struggle to trace where data comes from, how it is transformed, and if it is even used by business systems. When these systems involve AI applications then the challenge grows in impact. Without visibility and control around data sources (Note: data lineage= spices trade routes), AI models will be flying blind. Just as desire for spice shaped historic global trade routes, car parts supply sourcing is negotiated across hundreds of OEMs. The AI systems depend on the careful orchestration of diverse, owned or acquired, and dynamic data sources. The quality of any AI solution is only as strong as the data foundation it is built on. Also known as GIGO: Garbage in, Garbage out.

What is a Data Supply Chain?

A 'Farm to Table' supply chains is a familiar example that impacts our daily lives. Food consumption brings our low threshold of tolerance to the quality, the sourcing, the ownership and many other measures under scrutiny. We tend to be picky, curious and are constantly educating ourselves about what we eat. Improper harvesting and collection from the fields and neglected cleaning protocols can introduce bacteria into the food supply chain. The bacteria travelling with the food impacts the quality of food eaten by the consumer.

Likewise, data quality starts at the very point of its creation or ingestion into an organization. Errors and negligence to tag, cleanse, or organize the raw data sources will magnify the quality issues downstream.

Consider your reactions when Amazon recommends pool toys when you are searching for living room furniture. AI algorithms that made the recommendations do not always know your preferences. Early Amazon recommendation models would often suggest products that you had just finished buying or products that did not reflect your purchasing patterns. Over time the streamlining of data pattern quality fed to the model allowed Amazon to manage this issue better.

Google maps in east Asia are still problematic because street names and routes in these regions are not standardized. Better data collection and route documentation by GRAB made for superior transportation logistics algorithms, more relevant than google maps, for GRAB's services (GRAB 2024). The inability to present quality standardized information impacted the outcomes of the AI-route mapping in Asia.

Strategic Insight: Resilient Data Supply Chain

A robust data supply chain is the foundation for trustworthy, high-impact AI. Just as manufacturers embed quality assurance into every stage of production, organizations must do the same with their data from sourcing to consumption.

A data supply chain includes:

- **Data Production:** Source systems, IoT, transactions
- **Data Processing:** ETL/ELT pipelines, enrichment, transformation
- **Data Storage:** Warehouses, lakes, real-time buffers
- **Data Delivery**: APIs, dashboards, AI training sets
- **AI-Data Consumption**: Generation of Insights, recommendations, predictions
- **Business Outcomes:** Quality Products or services, Marketing & sales, Operational efficiency

Aligning your data supply chain to business use cases builds trust, transparency, and accelerates time-to-value for AI investments. To do this effectively, leaders must ask:

- What data is essential?
- Where does it originate?
- How is it transformed?
- Who relies on it and for what decisions?

Understanding these dimensions ensures that data quality, metadata, and traceability are not afterthoughts but integral components at every stage of the supply chain. In an AI-enabled enterprise, your data supply chain is not just a technical backbone. It is a **strategic differentiator**.

Use Cases

Automotive:
AI-Driven Supply Chain Optimization at GM

General Motors (GM) (Kelly 2024) offers a compelling example of a modern data supply chain designed to fuel AI. Facing risks across its extensive supplier network, GM deployed predictive AI tools and machine learning models to monitor supply chain health and proactively address risks.

One such tool, the 'Supplier Home Dashboard,' provides real-time risk ratings for suppliers. It enables GM to detect early signs of potential disruption and intervention before production is affected. This was especially critical during its transition to electric vehicle (EV) manufacturing.

In parallel, GM partnered with Optilogic to deploy 'Cosmic Frog,' a software platform that enhances supply chain visibility across SKUs and supplier tiers, supporting predictive simulations (Stroh 2024).

These systems rely on well-curated, real-time data inputs from ERP, logistics, and quality control systems. The output? Faster insights, risk prevention, and a more agile, resilient supply chain.

Lesson: To make effective decisions we need quality data at each point of the 'product' supply chain. Data itself is changing and transforming at each of those hand-off points. Managing the data supply chain is a prerequisite to managing your product supply chain.

Executive Reflection

To transform data into actionable insights, recommendation, or strategic content, evaluating the Data-to-Insights Pipeline is part of the critical path for your organization.

1. Do you understand where your critical data comes from (e.g., customer support interactions, purchase frequency) to deliver the insights?

2. Can you trace how it is processed and transformed?

3. Are you monitoring the quality and timeliness of our data sources?

4. What actions can you take to improve the alignment of insights with business goals?

Call to Action: Map Data Supply Chain

For a key AI use case, map the following:

- Raw data sources
- Processing and transformation steps
- Storage systems and formats
- Distribution mechanisms (e.g., APIs, reports)
- Final consumption points (dashboards, AI models)
- Known gaps in traceability, governance, or timeliness

This simple map becomes your data supply chain for the AI initiative.

Summary

Just like in manufacturing or agriculture, transforming raw materials into high-quality output requires a well-designed supply chain. In the world of AI, this means having traceable, reliable, and timely flows of data that connect to business use cases. The data supply chain analogy helps leaders conceptualize how insights are produced and where quality can break down.

Lessons Learned

- A strong AI data pipeline requires intentional design, traceability, and business alignment at every stage.
- Quality of ingested data will impact the quality of data used along the supply chain.
- Data must be managed with the same rigor as physical inputs in a supply chain.
- Small and mid-sized businesses can leapfrog by focusing on their data transformation path, not just their tools.
- Understanding and mapping of your data supply chain can reveal gaps in governance, readiness, and reuse.

EMBED FEEDBACK LOOPS

Chapter 3: Managing a New Asset Class of Generated Data

"What AI creates must be governed just like what

AI consumes."

Where is new data being generated?

With the rise of generative AI, organizations are producing more data than ever before, such as summaries, synthetic training data, email drafts, images, videos, and more. This generated data is powerful, but also complex. It introduces a new category of assets that must be managed with intentionality and care.

Unlike raw transactional or structured data, generated content often bypasses traditional governance processes. It is created on-demand, frequently shared ad hoc, and may include hallucinations, biases, or outdated content. As AI-generated assets begin influencing decisions, communication, and products, businesses must recognize this content as strategic and govern it accordingly.

The challenge of recognizing deepfakes is both real and personal. From identity theft using manipulated images and voices, to fabricated video consent and scam advertisements, malicious use of AI-generated content has reached alarming levels of sophistication.

One of the most high-profile examples occurred in early 2024, when AI-generated explicit images of singer Taylor Swift were widely circulated on social media. The post was shared across major media and social platforms like X. There was a global outrage and a call for stricter platform regulation. The incident brought heightened awareness to four critical concerns:

- Violation of personal dignity through the misuse of AI-generated content.
- Inadequate content governance and oversight on mainstream social media platforms.
- Failure of proactive detection and monitoring systems, even for high-profile individuals.
- The urgent need for enforceable AI governance frameworks to address synthetic media risks.

These abuses not only pose ethical and legal risks; they also contaminate publicly available data with synthetic and often toxic inputs. Large language models (LLMs) are trained on vast digital corpora, much of which originates from internet sources like publications, forums, blogs, and social media. If this data is polluted with manipulated or misleading content, it can distort the outputs of AI models in subtle yet impactful ways. This is commonly referred to as "hallucination", where AI generates confident but inaccurate responses. As organizations adopt generative AI at scale, they must proactively address the origins, quality, and governance of the data that feeds their models.

The Big Problem

Most organizations lack policies, tools, and training to govern the lifecycle of generated data. Without classification, auditability, and risk scoring, it becomes difficult to verify which outputs can be reused, which require review, and which may cause harm or misinformation if distributed. Despite the rapid adoption of generative AI, many organizations lack robust policies and frameworks to govern the lifecycle of AI-generated content. Without proper classification, auditability, and risk assessment, there's a heightened risk of misinformation, bias propagation, and compliance breaches.

Strategic Insight: Generated Data as a First-Class Asset

To manage generated data effectively, organizations must integrate it into their existing data governance programs. This includes:

- **Classifying** generated content by type (e.g., internal, public-facing, PII-sensitive)
- **Setting review policies** (e.g., human-in-the-loop verification for high-risk outputs)
- **Tagging and storing** outputs with metadata
- **Tracking prompts,** models used, and timestamps for compliance
- **Establishing audit trails** and access logs to monitor usage and modifications

21

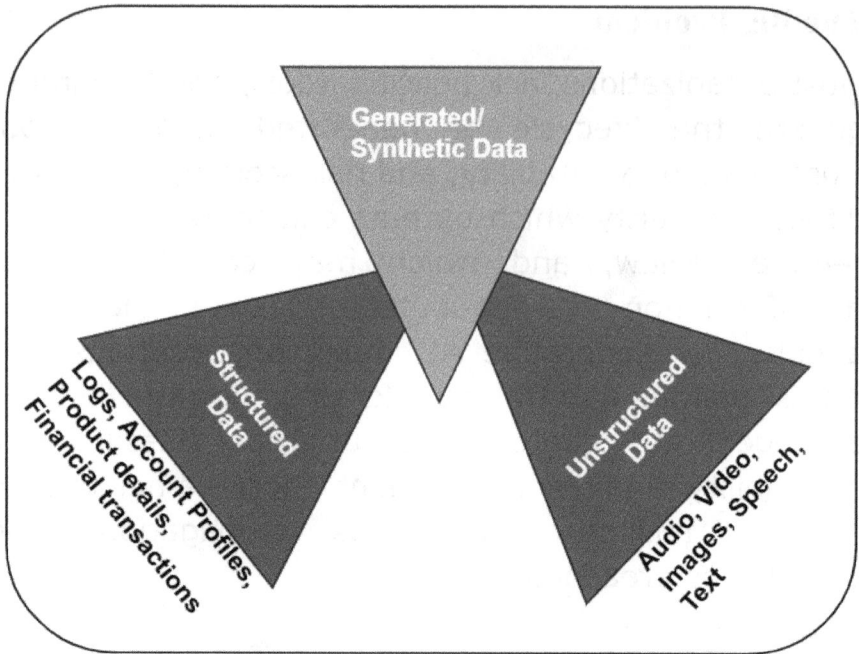

Figure 5: Generated Data Assets

Ignoring this data governance challenge puts businesses at risk. Not just of poor decision-making, but of compliance lapses, reputational harm, and hidden biases perpetuated at scale by the unmonitored generated data assets.

To lead AI responsibly, organizations must begin treating generated data as a first-class asset, with the same level of governance, quality, and accountability applied to traditionally sourced data.

Use Cases

Legal:

The integration of AI in legal processes has seen various implementations:

- Anthropic's Claude API: Provides capabilities for summarizing legal documents, aiding in efficient legal analysis
- Spellbook: Utilizes AI to highlight and extract key facts from legal documents, streamlining the review process.
- Clio's AI Tools: Offers AI-driven legal document review to automate processes and enhance eDiscovery.

These use cases, from legal document review to eDiscovery, (Chalmers 2025) (Neumeister 2025) illustrate just how quickly organizations are integrating AI-generated content into core operations. But while the focus has long been on preparing data for AI, we're now entering a new era where **AI becomes a producer of data**. This shift brings new questions:

- Who owns the generated output?
- How reliable is it?
- Can we audit and trace it?

Lesson: Governance and monitoring of AI-generated data must be treated as foundational requirements and not as optional features for any AI tool or automation process. Without oversight, the risks of misinformation, bias, and compliance failures multiply as AI scales.

Executive Reflection

Understanding the data-information pipeline that connects the raw data to the business goals is important to tag the points at which new data or information is being generated. One should think through how to extend AI data governance to new generated data to ensure trust in data quality.

1. What types of content are being generated by AI in your organization?

2. Do you know who uses and distributes this content?

3. Are there policies in place to review, track, and secure it?

Call to Action: Classify Generated Content

List examples of generated content in your department or function. For each, consider:

- What system or tool is generating it?
- Is it used internally or shared externally?
- What risk level does it carry?
- Who is responsible for its review and storage?
- Is it tagged or traceable after creation?

Summary

As generative AI becomes mainstream, the data it produces is growing rapidly and unpredictably. Generated data is no longer a novelty. It is an emerging asset class with its own quality, risk, and governance requirements. Organizations must begin to treat this data as strategically as any traditional enterprise dataset. That means there is a critical need to create metadata for traceability, labeling it for risk, validating its purpose, and evaluating its fitness-for-use. Governance for generated data must evolve to include both the origin (e.g., prompt or model) and the output (e.g., image, summary, recommendation).

Lessons Learned

- Generated data is a strategic asset, not just a byproduct.
- Governance must account for both input prompt and output integrity.
- Generated content should be labeled, risk-rated, and tracked.
- Data quality frameworks must evolve to evaluate generated outputs.
- Managing AI-generated data is not just technical, it is legal, ethical, and operational.

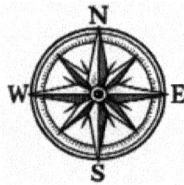

GOVERN FOR TRUST

Chapter 4: Structuring and Governing AI-Grade Data

"Your AI is only as good as your weakest dataset."

Having data is not enough. For AI systems, especially those driven by machine learning and generative models, data must be structured, contextualized, and governed with purpose. Transforming raw information into AI-ready assets is no longer a technical task delegated to IT (Information Technology) teams, it is a strategic responsibility for business leadership.

Building on the data supply chain introduced in the last chapter, we have already emphasized the importance of aligning data quality actions with business outcomes. But that alignment must now go further: **the clarity of your use case** must directly inform the standards for how data is ingested, transformed, and validated to support the AI approach in use.

Not all data is created equal, and neither are the expectations tied to it. The level of accuracy, completeness or standardization required will vary by use case. For instance, projecting financial metrics demands highly accurate data to inform a firm's valuation and growth strategy. If your AI models are trained on incomplete data or ignore training-related infrastructure costs, like productivity dips or resource consumption, you risk producing misleading forecasts that derail budget and strategy.

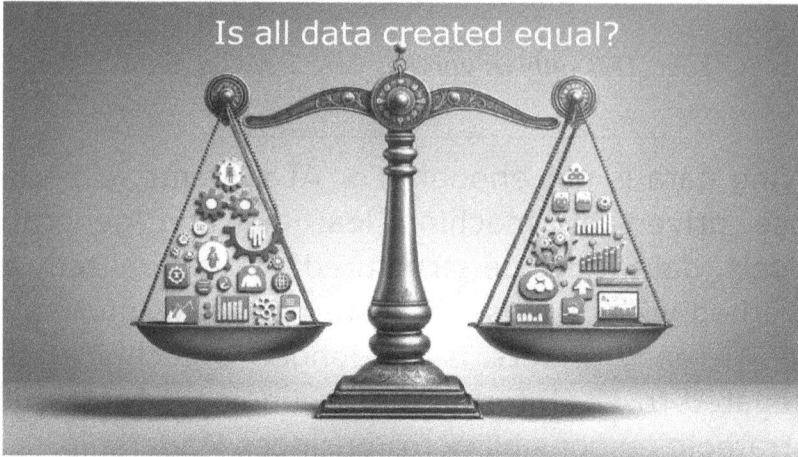
Is all data created equal?

Even within a single use case, quality expectations shift by industry or maturity. Think of it like sourcing potatoes: a fast-food chain prioritizes consistency and shelf life; a Michelin-starred restaurant demands traceability, texture, and taste. The same ingredient but radically different expectations.

This is why effective data governance starts with identifying the **relevant use case**. Traditional centralized governance under a Chief Data Officer (CDO) works well for managed, structured sources. But as AI expands, data becomes more **federated and generative**. Governing these modern flows requires deep domain insight, decentralized accountability, and adaptive policies.

Perhaps it is time to introduce a 4-star Michelin rating system, not just for restaurants, but for enterprise data. As AI systems become more embedded in decision-making, we need a way to assess not only data quality, but its contextual relevance and readiness for high stakes use.

Consider a CRM platform. When used to power AI-led chatbots interacting with customers, data quality becomes paramount, affecting tone, personalization, and ultimately, the customer's perception of your brand. In contrast, a generic email campaign announcing a new product feature may rely on the same dataset, but the reputational risk of a few bad email addresses is far lower.

Not all data needs the same quality scrutiny, but the scrutiny must match the stakes. Organizations must adopt a more nuanced, use-case-aware approach to data quality; prioritizing precision where AI decisions are public-facing, regulated, or strategic, and scaling effort appropriately elsewhere.

The Big Problem

Many AI projects fail not because the algorithms are flawed, but because the data they rely on is incomplete, inconsistent, or unstructured. Without well-prepared data, AI systems hallucinate, underperform, or make biased decisions. Data governance is often underdeveloped or disconnected from AI initiatives, creating critical gaps in lineage, quality, and accountability. As AI programs scale, so must the governing structures. The use of a decentralized and federated approach to data governance is one way to respond to the complexity of an enterprise scale AI program and to recognize the value it is likely to deliver.

Here is a mapping of AI data quality requirements tiers against some sample use cases.

Table 1: Data Quality Tiering Framework

Tier	Use Case	Data Quality Requirements	Governance Approach
Critical	AI Chatbots, Credit decisioning, medical diagnosis	Very high accuracy, traceability, real time freshness, compliance	Strict policies, HITL validations, audits and model logs
High	Customer segmentation, dynamic pricing, Fraud detection	High accuracy, contextual relevance, clear metadata tagging	Governed by domain stewards and monitored periodically
Moderate	Email Campaigns, Internal dashboards, Trend analysis	Moderate- Basic cleaning, Deduplication acceptable freshness	Light governance with thresholds for alert triggers
Low	A/B testing variants, social Media monitoring, data exploration	Low – minimal cleaning, exploratory use, low operational risk	Ad hoc or automated rules, minimal human oversight

Strategic Insight: What Makes Data AI-Grade?

AI-grade data must be:

- **Standardized**: Common formats, units, and naming conventions
- **Labeled:** Annotated to support machine learning models
- **Auditable:** Traceable with clear lineage and provenance
- **Governed:** Owned, validated, and quality-controlled by responsible teams
- **Integrable:** Easy to discover, accessed by AI-pipelines, usable

The FAIR data principles, first articulated by Wilkinson et al. (Wilkinson 2016), invoke the need for data to be Findable, Accessible, Interoperable/Integrable and Reusable. These features are relevant to the class of AI-generated data.

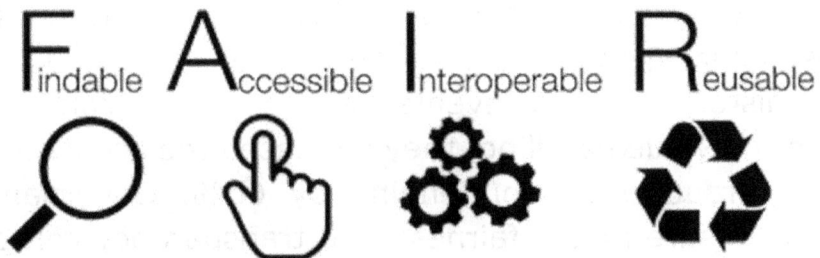

Figure 6 The FAIR Principle of Data Classification

FAIR principles can be summarized as follows:

Findable: To reuse data, the data should be easy to find by both humans and machines.

Accessible: Once found, users' need to access, authenticate, and be authorized to extract for integration.

Interoperable: Once extracted, the data needs to be integrated with other data, applications, and workflows to allow analysis, storage, and processing.

Reusable: The value of data is optimized by creating awareness, tools, documentation, and training that allow new use cases to be driven by reusing data.

Use Cases

Financial Services:
Fraud Detection in Financial Services

MSU credit union (Pindrop 2024) wanted to build a fraud scoring system but faced highly inconsistent transaction logs across different channels. By harmonizing schema definitions, applying labeled tags to historical fraud events, and creating rules for missing value handling, they increased the accuracy of their fraud prediction engine by 60%. Governance tools ensure model fairness and transparency comply with financial regulations.

Fintech:

Identity Verification and Fraud Prevention in FinTech FinTech companies increasingly lose up to 9% of revenue to fraud, as estimated by LexisNexis and GAO reports. In response, one digital lender implemented an AI-driven identity authentication system to detect fraud before it reached the transaction layer (Synapse 2025).

The AI system ingested data across multiple dimensions—financial, demographic, and behavioral, and utilized global entity mapping to enrich feature sets. The data governance strategy focused on:

- Timely entity resolution using global IDs
- Real-time scoring with SLAs measured in milliseconds
- Contextual feature extraction from multiple domains
- Transparent output tracking for legal and compliance needs
- Feedback loops and model explainability integrated from the start

By embedding governance into the end-to-end data flow, they reduced false positives, improved customer onboarding experience, and met regulatory expectations around algorithmic transparency.

Lesson: Data quality is not one-size-fits-all. Different use cases demand different governance standards that must align to the risk tier of each use case. Monitoring and feedback loops are prerequisites for deploying AI solutions, particularly when data is generated.

Executive Reflection

Prioritizing the data governance structures based on the importance and criticality of the AI initiative is key to getting started on building the foundation for AI-grade systems. For this cross-functional team involvement is important through the formation of workgroups, AI boards, or joint AI governance collaborations.

1.   Is your data being curated with AI use in mind?

2.   Do you have governance roles defined for your most critical datasets?

3.   Are you actively auditing your data quality and lineage before feeding AI models?

Call to Action: AI Grade Data Readiness

Select a high-priority AI use case and assess the following for the key datasets involved:

- Are data needs standardized across business?
- Have they been labeled for supervised learning or classification?

- Is there documentation on data lineage and transformation steps?
- What governance process ensures ongoing quality and accountability?

Summary

AI-grade data does not happen by accident. It requires structure, governance, and alignment with the intended use case. This chapter explores the traits of high-quality machine-usable data. It emphasized the need for decentralized domain-aware governance to scale AI successfully. As AI use cases become more complex, the threshold for data readiness, labeling, standardization, auditability, become even more critical.

Lessons Learned

- AI-grade data must be standardized, labeled, auditable, and governed—tailored to the needs of the AI it supports.
- Use case clarity sets the quality bar; different applications demand different levels of data quality and governance rigor.
- Traditional centralized governance must evolve into federated models with domain ownership and accountability.
- The FAIR data principles (Findable, Accessible, Interoperable, Reusable) provide a strong

foundation for scaling AI-ready data across business units.

- Without structured data governance, advanced AI models will underperform or produce biased outcomes.

GOVERN FOR TRUST, NOT JUST CONTROL

Chapter 5: Data That Scales Value

"Strategic data multiplies its return across use cases."

In the journey from proof of concept (POC) to enterprise-wide AI transformation, one pattern becomes clear: the organizations that scale value are the ones that have designed data for reuse and not just for one-time use.

As established in Chapters 1 through 4, building a successful AI strategy hinges on treating data as a foundational asset. We've explored why strategic data matters (Chapter 1), how it flows through the enterprise like a supply chain (Chapter 2), the emergence of AI-generated content (Chapter 3), and the transformation of raw data into AI-grade assets (Chapter 4). This chapter brings these elements together to focus on the true multiplier effect of data— its ability to scale value when it is reused, enriched, and aligned with evolving business use cases.

This culminates in a pivotal question for leaders:

How do we scale the value of data, rather than simply scaling the volume of AI?

The typical journey begins with a proof of concept (POC), advances through operationalization before considering enterprise-wide scaling. It begins with a strong data foundation.

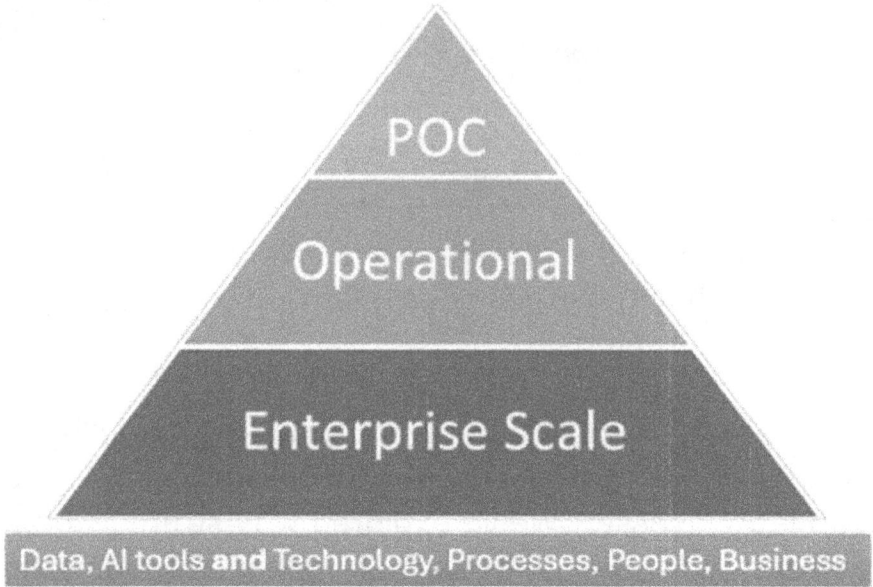

Figure 7: Simple Enterprise Scaling Journey

From Assets to Products

When data is curated to support multiple models, teams, or decisions, it evolves into a 'Data Product', **a versioned, documented, and owned entity designed for reuse**. Scaling value is not about having more data; it is about creating assets that serve multiple AI initiatives with traceability and trust.

Creating data assets that bring together structured and unstructured data along with a common enterprise ontology allows AI to explore the potential use cases of data further to develop new revenue lines. At scale, the same dataset may fuel assistants, agents, automation pipelines, and decision systems.

From a governance perspective, a data product foundation allows for efficiency in version control, contextual layering, and alignment with enterprise risk frameworks.

The Big Problem

Organizations often fall into the trap of building bespoke data pipelines for every new AI initiative. These isolated efforts lead to **duplication, inconsistency, and waste**. Rather than leveraging trusted data assets across multiple use cases, teams rebuild from scratch, slowing progress and limiting impact. Valuable datasets sit idle, documentation is sparse, and institutional knowledge is lost in the shuffle.

This siloed approach not only drives up costs, but it also undermines confidence in the data itself. In AT&T CDO Andy Markus's (Andy Markus 2023) words:

" Making sense of our data really maximizes the reuse of our data, if we do things twice, we're just wasting money. Let's find the right way to do it."

- Andy Markus, CDO AT&T

This perspective underscores a foundational truth that data reused at scale demands a **connected architecture**. Without it, the burden of rebuilding datasets, retraining models, and replicating pipelines grows exponentially, eroding both trust and efficiency.

True data reuse requires **connected ecosystems** including the following key features:

- Cloud-native Platforms
- Governed Metadata Layers
- Shared Semantic Models
- Performance Monitoring

This allows the same data to serve diverse use cases with minimal rework.

Strategic Insight: Design for Reuse

To scale value with data:
- **Design for reuse:** Separate raw from modeled layers to enable flexible use downstream
- **Document thoroughly**: Use metadata, lineage, and context tracking to build trust and amplify discoverability.
- **Think product:** Treat curated datasets as internal products with defined owners, SLAs, lifecycle plans
- **Aligning to business metrics:** Demonstrate how datasets contribute to multiple outcomes like sales retention, cost reduction etc.

Start with business and not with the AI tool. Avoid the trap of retrofitting AI into an existing system. Select the tools for the data that can respond best to the business objectives. A gap assessment of the compatibility with the AI tools selected and the timelines for delivery should be done to assess the technical debt vs. new investment decision.

Use Case

Retail Banking:
Intelligent Customer Support in Retail Banking

This retail banking example illustrates a powerful truth: **the value of data doesn't come from its quantity but from how it is governed, reused, and extended across business needs.**

Initially, there existed a knowledge base, customer support transactions, logs around escalation, conversation captured to text, that supported internal customer service agents. With maturing data governance practices, the data was catalogued and repurposed to roll out and power an AI-driven chatbot for external customer engagement. The same structured artifacts were adapted, tested, and audited for real-time chatbot responses. Over time, this generated response data that became the basis for training new staff, answering compliance queries, identifying customer pain points, improving online tagging, FAQs anticipating customer queries and even building predictive models on customer inquiry trends.

That's the promise of a reuse-first mindset. When teams invest in organizing, documenting, and stewarding their data, they unlock a multiplier effect. One that fuels more than just a single use case (Priya Sarathy 2024).

Executive Reflection

As your organization moves beyond one-off AI experiments, the ability to scale value depends on whether your data can serve many without being rebuilt each time. These questions are designed to help you evaluate if your data assets and your strategy are ready for that next level of performance.

- Are you creating datasets designed for single use or multiple strategic purposes?
- Do you track and manage data reuse across business functions?
- Have you built metadata and cataloguing systems to support data discoverability?

Call to Action: Assess Data Reusability

Pick one high-value dataset in your organization. For that dataset, answer:

- Who created and owned this dataset?

- What was its original purpose or use case?
- Has it been used by more than one team or project?
- Is it documented in a catalog or metadata system?
- What additional use cases could this data serve with small modifications?

Summary

This chapter emphasizes the strategic advantage of designing data for reuse, rather than single-use applications. Organizations that scale AI value do so by treating data as a product: well-documented, governed, and aligned with multiple business use cases. When curated datasets can support diverse AI models, decision systems, and customer experiences, data shifts from being a static asset to a dynamic multiplier.

Lessons Learned

- Scaling AI value depends on building reusable, high-quality data assets.
- Data products should be versioned, cataloged, and governed like software products.
- Reuse reduces duplication and amplifies return on data investments across teams.
- Platform thinking, shared infrastructure, discoverability, and lineage are essential to sustain data reuse.
- Cross-functional data stewardship enhances both adoption and accountability.

MEASURE WHAT MATTERS

Chapter 6: The Human-in-the-Loop Imperative

"AI without humans is automation.

AI with humans is augmentation."

As AI systems scale across industries, one truth becomes undeniable: their success depends on meaningful human involvement. While AI excels at computing speed, consistency of reasoning, and pattern recognition, it still lacks the context, ethical judgment, and the human intuition needed for responsible decision-making. Human-in-the-loop (HITL) models ensure that AI systems are guided, corrected, and complemented by expert oversight. Introducing and building human relatable empathy into the AI design is still work-in-progress.

Consider your skill growth from a child to an adult or your professional skill growth from an entry level candidate to your current role as a ranking manager. AI in contrast, is still a young teen needing parental guidance to participate effectively in society or a young professional working on mastering skills and domain knowledge to survive in the corporate world. This supports the fact that AI needs continuous supervision, coaching, and guidance.

This chapter explores how HITL is implemented in different industries, the rationale behind it, and the structures that make it successful. From retail merchandising to healthcare diagnostics and manufacturing inspection, HITL plays a pivotal role not just in ensuring safety and accuracy, but in driving collaboration, trust, and adoption.

The Big Problem

Automation and AI systems promise enormous gains in efficiency, consistency, and cost savings. But in the rush to scale these systems, many organizations are skipping a critical step: **preparing their people to stay in control**. Strategic decisions, talent development, customer trust, and ethical alignment all require human insight that no **current** AI system can replicate those tasks. Efficiency is not the only measure or even the most important measure of success. Strategic thinking, talent development, ethical decisions, and customer trust still rely on human insight, judgment, and oversight. These are needed to support organizational value creation.

An imbalance can lead to high-profile setbacks. Klarna (Hari 2025), for instance, replaced over 700 workers with AI only to suffer a $40 billion drop in market value, demonstrating that **AI maturity alone does not guarantee business maturity.** Even with advanced systems, decisions about human oversight remain contextual, sensitive, and often irreversible.

One truth is evident: *Organizations are automating AI and systems faster than they are preparing humans to be able to remain in control.*

The real challenge is not just about keeping a human "in the loop." It is about deciding when, where, and how human intervention should be embedded based on the level of risk, explainability, and cultural readiness.

Figure 8 (Dion 2020) illustrates how human roles span across the AI lifecycle—from casual users on the left to technical architects on the right. This spectrum reflects not just skill levels, but degrees of interaction, risk, and accountability.

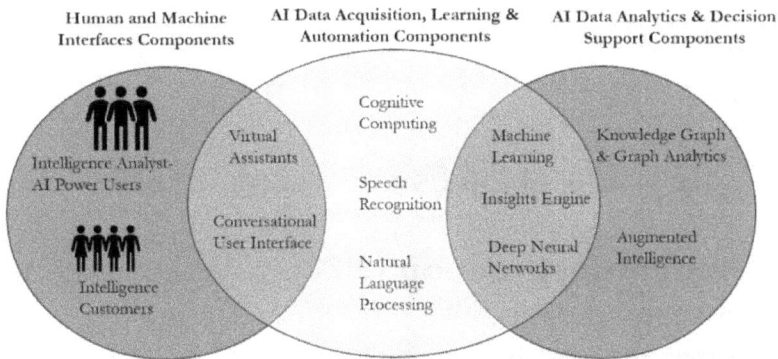

Figure 8: Human Roles in AI Ecosystem

- On the left, democratized AI tools empower customers and analysts with guided insights. But they still require training and awareness of risks, bias, and overreach.
- In the center, AI enablers (like digital assistants, prompt engineers, and data translators) act as a

bridge between intuitive interfaces and sophisticated algorithms.
- On the right, expert practitioners oversee algorithm design, model performance, and impact. The role requires advanced technical fluency and business context awareness.

Governance frameworks, like those from the National Institute of Standards and Technology (NIST) (NIST 2023) remind us that responsible AI is not just a systems problem, it is a **human judgment challenge**. Organizations must decide.

- When do humans need to approve AI outputs?
- When is real-time monitoring sufficient?
- And when, **if ever**, can decisions be fully automated?

Three core models help us understand this:

- **Human-in-the-loop (HITL):** AI recommends, humans decide.
- **Human-on-the-loop:** AI acts autonomously, humans supervise.
- **Human-out-of-the-loop:** AI acts independently, without direct human oversight.

The right model is not purely technical. It must reflect your risk appetite, explainability requirements, cultural values, and readiness to respond. Embedding human roles strategically is what keeps automation aligned with purpose and the organizations aligned with trust.

Use Cases
Cross-Industry Use Human-AI Collaboration

Retail: H&M merchandisers (Alaimo 2018) partnered with data scientists to **co-develop** pricing algorithms. Their domain expertise improved the models' market fit and ensured cultural buy-in. Here, HITL served as both algorithmic tuning and organizational change. Using AI on the front end to automate customer experience and in the backend leaning on human – **co-design, co-development, and final trend selection.**

Healthcare: In radiology and robotic surgery, AI **assists** in anomaly detection and precision execution, but radiologists and trained surgeons make the final decisions. The Da Vinci system (Patel 2024) translates the surgeon's hand movements at the console in real time, bending and rotating the instruments while performing the procedure. The tiny wristed instruments move like a human hand but with a greater range of motion.

Surgical AI systems like the Da Vinci Robot are supervised by surgeons, in real-time, showcase the human-on-the-loop model. Where **AI augments but never replaces real-time medical judgment**.

Human Resources: Walmart and Delta deploy AI Aware (Field 2024) to detect and monitor cyber bullying, harassment, discrimination, noncompliance, pornography, nudity and other behaviors among employees. Here, AI **triggers detection**, but **humans retain control over consequences**—a critical balance in sensitive workplace contexts.

Legal: Law departments using GenAI to summarize contracts and **mandate a human review** layer to verify interpretations, particularly for risk clauses and legal language nuances. This mitigates AI hallucinations and reinforces legal accountability.

HITL and Responsible AI Governance

Each of these examples illustrates a central lesson: **Human involvement must be intentional, contextual, and strategic.** It is not just about placing a person at the end of a pipeline—it is about embedding human judgment, transparency, and accountability **throughout** the AI lifecycle.

Frameworks like the **NIST AI Risk Management Framework** and the author's **RADAR approach (Read – Ask – Document – Aware – Report)** underscore this need. As AI innovation accelerates, **case-based education, contextual review, and professional ethics** become essential—not optional.

This idea is expanded in Chapter 13, but the foundation is clear here: responsible AI governance begins with **thoughtful human design, not after-the-fact correction.**

Executive Reflection

"AI demands even greater responsibility from companies like ours."

- Satya Nadella, CEO Microsoft Inc.

Source: (Microsoft 2023)

By collaborating and spearheading Office Co-Pilot with OpenAI, Microsoft took the lead in recognizing the need and have provided extensive frameworks and tools for users to review, assess and manage these new human-AI responsibilities.

Community, society, and nations are human-centric organizations that exhibit diverse levels of empathy, emotional balance, and viewpoints. There is always an opportunity for dissent and veto. In a business, the vision, scope, and goals are more clearly stated. This allows for greater flexibility to adapt and use AI.

As AI systems grow in scope and scale, ask yourself

1. Where is human judgment essential in your AI workflows?

2. Who is accountable for reviewing and validating AI decisions?

3. Are the HITL mechanisms formalized, measured, and improved over time?

4. Have you trained staff to engage effectively with AI systems?

Call to Action: Map HITL Touchpoints

For a key AI initiative in your organization, identify:
- What decisions do AI make or recommend?
- Where and when human intervention is expected?
- Who is responsible for final review and accountability?
- What safeguards are in place to escalate or override poor decisions?
- How is feedback incorporated to improve model applications to meet those goals?

Summary

This chapter emphasizes the critical role of human oversight in AI systems. Rather than replacing human judgment, successful AI implementations augment it, ensuring ethical standards, context awareness, and accountability are preserved.

Human-in-the-loop (HITL) models reinforce trust and reduce risks across decision-making processes—from healthcare and legal review to automated monitoring systems.

Lessons Learned

- HITL frameworks are essential for responsible AI use in high-risk domains.
- Human judgment should guide AI outputs, especially where ethical, legal, or contextual nuances matter.
- Clear roles and accountability must be defined for reviewing and approving AI-generated decisions.
- HITL design supports transparency, bias mitigation, and user confidence in AI outputs. Organizations must train personnel to interpret and intervene in AI workflows effectively.

ORCHESTRATE, DO NOT COMMAND

Chapter 7: Building AI Fluency

"If your people are not ready for AI, your business is not either."

As AI initiatives mature from proof of concept to scaled operations, one of the most cited barriers to success is not data or technology, it is people. Specifically, a lack of AI fluency across roles, functions, and leadership levels. From warehouse technicians to senior executives, everyone needs to understand how AI changes their workflows, decisions, and value creation responsibilities.

This chapter explores what it means to build AI fluency, how to tailor learning paths for different audiences, and why organizational upskilling must be both inclusive and intentional.

Drawing inspiration from **Stephen Covey's** (Covey 2004) principle-centered leadership, AI fluency must start with mindset before method. Covey's habit of "Sharpening the Saw" (Habit #7) reminds us that continuous learning is not a luxury. It is a necessity. In the AI era, sharpening the **AI Saw** means cultivating curiosity, building awareness of emerging technologies, and encouraging individuals at every level to challenge their assumptions. Upskilling is not just about technical know-how; it is about developing proactive habits, ethical grounding, and adaptability that allow individuals to thrive alongside intelligent machines and systems.

There is often confusion between AI literacy and AI fluency. Data scientists have long been seen as technically adept but "lacking business acumen." I would argue that this was less of a shortcoming of the data scientists, and more a failure of business leaders to understand the language of analytics. Today, AI literacy is widely accessible through videos, podcasts, and online courses. But literacy only gets you so far. Fluency is the practical ability to apply AI in context, understanding when, where, and why it is valuable.

The Big Problem

Have you ever taken a class on how to cut vegetables? Why do knife skills matter? Why do brands like Sheffield, Wüsthof, or Misono hold such high value?

Because knowledge about the right tool can turn food preparation into a work of art. Knives used incorrectly can still cause injury. Understanding how to use AI tools is only one part of the equation. True AI fluency means applying them responsibly, verifying outputs, understanding business impacts, and questioning how models are trained.

If you have trained yourself in basic knife techniques to cut safely and precisely. That is AI literacy. However, access to tools does not equal fluency. AI fluency is more nuanced. It is knowing which knife to use: a paring knife to peel an apple or a bread knife to slice a loaf. Fluency brings confidence and awareness about tool application and its **intentional use.**

Table 2: AI Literacy vs. AI Fluency

Dimension	AI LITERACY	AI FLUENCY
Definition	Foundational awareness of what AI is, how it works in principle, and where it is applied	Practical ability to apply AI knowledge in context to make better decisions that improve workflows
Cognitive Depth	Recognition, recall, and comprehension of key AI terms, risks, and categories	Application, synthesis, and judgement in AI-supported tasks and strategic impact in AI-generated insights
Learning Objective	Understand the terminology, capabilities, risks, and societal impact of AI	Use AI tools, interpret results, integrate outputs, and make decisions grounded in AI generated insights
Comparable To	Reading AI-related content and engaging in informed conversation	Speaking and collaborating fluently using AI as a business enabler
Audience	General staff, risk and compliance teams, operations, policy stakeholders	Product owners, functional leaders, strategy, marketing, analytics teams
Typical Roles	Customer service, HR generalist, project managers, early-stage learners	Business analysts, marketing leads, data-savvy executives, transformation leads
Training Focus	What is AI, where it fits, basic risks and ethical implications	How to frame AI use cases, evaluate model performances, and collaborate with technical partners
Content Format	Awareness videos, gamified learning, 101 workshops, simulation of basic prompts and their outcomes	Can use or apply AI tools for insight generation, flagging anomalies, supporting professional productivity or quality
Use of Tools	Understands and awareness about the different AI tools, features and general context of use	Applies responsible AI practices within role: verifying outputs, understanding business impacts, questioning training

The above table summarizes different dimensions of AI fluency.

Capability Gaps and Cultural Resistance

Many organizations assume that introducing AI tools will naturally drive productivity. However, tooling without training only breeds frustration and underutilization. Without a plan for upskilling, organizations face an AI fluency gap: where strategy outpaced execution. This results in failed deployments, disengaged teams, and limited innovation.

Closing the AI fluency gap starts with tailored learning, delivered in context, not just in courses.

This reflection exposes a harsh truth: the bottleneck to innovation is not always technical capability; it is leadership capacity. If leaders remain stuck in old decision cycles, AI becomes a wasted investment. The leaders who thrive will be those who embrace transparency, accountability, and experimentation, not just control. AI fluency builds awareness and perspectives for leaders to manage the most valuable resources, the people.

Without intentional upskilling around AI fluency:

- Frontline users resist adoption.
- Middle managers misinterpret or misunderstand model outputs.
- Executives fail to link AI insights to business goals.
- Responsible AI governance is an afterthought.

Despite the growing availability of self-service tools and automation, human understanding remains central to responsible AI use.

"AI is not the easy button—it's complexity is disguised under a simple interface of GenAI. "
- Leadership Compass

Strategic Insight: Tailor AI Learning Paths

AI fluency skills do not map to a checklist that can be completed with a course. Upskilling must be role-based, outcome-aligned, and embedded into daily workflows. Organizations seeking to close the AI fluency gap need to start with tailored learning, delivered in context, not just in courses. Here are eight best practices recommended by Dataiku based on Dataiku's "8 Steps for Leaders to Drive AI Literacy Success (Grasso 2025):

- Secure executive sponsorship
- Build a diverse team
- Perform assessments
- Define role-specific objectives
- Develop tailored content
- Track meaningful metrics
- Democratize access with governance
- Foster a culture of continuous learning

Across industries, leaders are embedding AI learning into workflows to drive both adoption and innovation by nurturing all around AI fluency.

Use Cases

Merchandisers: H&M (Marr 2018) integrated merchandisers in the algorithm development process to ensure AI models reflected fashion intuition and in-market relevance. This co-creation led to better adoption and created internal AI champions.

Healthcare Systems: Healthcare systems like Stanford Medicine (Floor Schuur 2021) introduced upskilling programs for medical coders and radiologists to interpret and validate AI-generated suggestions for patient charts and scans.

Distribution: Logistics and warehouse operations at Amazon Shreveport (Infra.com 2025), Louisiana, fulfillment center, use "AI shadowing" with new recruits. The facility employs over 750,000 mobile robots and tens of thousands of robotic arms to enhance efficiency and reduce delivery times. Despite the high level of automation, Amazon emphasizes the collaborative nature of its operations, where human workers and AI-powered machines work in tandem to optimize warehouse processes.

Lesson: AI fluency empowers leaders to guide co-design, co-creation, and co-innovation with HITL. As we discussed in Chapter 6, human-in-the-loop design requires more than workflow changes. It demands fluency at every level of the organization

Executive Reflection

Upskilling your teams is not a one-time project. It is an ongoing essential need. As you assess your readiness to scale AI, ask:

1. Have you mapped what AI fluency looks like for each role in our organization?
2. Is your current learning strategy designed to evolve with the AI maturity of our teams?
3. Do your leaders visibly model continuous AI learning?
4. Are you measuring applied fluency or just course completions?

Call to Action: Build AI Literacy Sprints

Identify 3 core AI skills needed in your department:

- Define the learning outcomes.
- Map a 3-week sprint with resources.
- Assign metrics (e.g., project pitch, post-training quiz).
- Identify 1–2 cultural blockers and plan mitigations.

Summary

As AI adoption expands, organizations must prioritize role-specific AI fluency. One-size-fits-all training models fail to prepare people for real-world interactions with intelligent systems. Upskilling must be iterative, governed, and embedded within both strategy and culture.

Lessons Learned

- AI fluency is a business enabler, not just a technical skill.
- Co-designing learning programs with business users increases relevance and adoption.
- AI literacy is a leadership imperative—leaders must model, sponsor, and participate in it.
- Measurable fluency drives responsible use, better decisions, and sustainable scale.

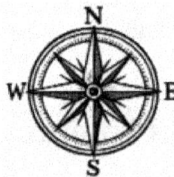

TRI-LINGUAL FLUENCY

Chapter 8: Empowering Users, Managing Risk

"Your AI is only as scalable as the people who know how to use it."

Until people overcame their fear of automation and discovered the thrill of driving, the popularity of automobiles (automated mobile units) remained limited. Owning a car was a luxury that upper-class individuals initially bought into. Self-propelled electric and gas vehicles appeared in the 1770s, but it wasn't until 1906 that France opened the first motorized bus line. Earlier, horse-drawn buses were used from the 1820s, followed by steam buses in the 1830s and electric trolleybuses in 1882.

Predictive AI, due to its complexity and skill demands, was entrusted to highly trained data scientists and engineers. With Generative Pre-Trained Transformers (GPT), access to AI has been democratized. Like automatic systems in cars, AI tools are now accessible to everyday users; easy to start yet requiring practice to navigate well. It took 50-60 years for automobiles to become popular and affordable. With GenAI, it took 5 days for OpenAI to register 1 million users, on ChatGPT, after its launch on Nov 30, 2022.

As organizations increasingly adopt AI, there is a growing need to scale AI training services to ensure users are equipped to interact with these technologies responsibly. **Fluency is what closes the gap**

between capability and responsibility. This chapter explores how Training-as-a-Service (TaaS) platforms facilitate scalable AI education while simultaneously addressing responsibility of managing user risk.

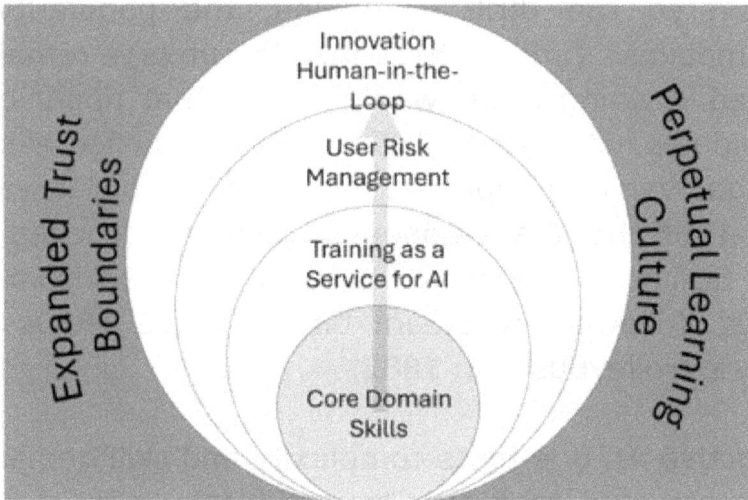

Figure 9: Scaling AI-Fluency

The Big Problem

Training for AI presents a classic "chicken and egg" dilemma. As organizations accelerate AI adoption across a variety of use cases, they face a key question:

Do we train for the tools we already have, or for the decisions we are about to empower with AI?

AI is **not a single system** with a predictable, standardized output. Its behavior varies dramatically depending on how it is aligned to the business problem, how it is deployed across functional domains, and how it is interpreted by the humans interacting with it. When users are not AI-fluent, the output of even the most sophisticated systems can be potentially misread, misused, or ignored.

To scale AI safely, organizations must build fluency from the inside out, starting with core domain knowledge, layering in literacy, and distributing training services that evolve with technology. But even as the AI systems and the users mature, **user-based risks persist** with AI-based tools.

These risks include:

- Over-relying on AI to replace domain expertise
- Mistaking probabilistic outputs for objective truth
- Acting on AI insights without human context or critical review

Untrained users do not just misuse AI, they misread its confidence as competence. To close this gap, training must evolve from generic onboarding to a dynamic, role-aware fluency strategy—one that grows alongside both the user and the system.

As AI tools are used, their outcomes can be observed, tested, and documented. These real-time interactions give users practical insight into the capabilities and limitations of AI systems. By measuring the business impact and the usage, leaders gain the ability to trace the data-AI decision chain. Iterations of observations and reflection deepen leadership fluency.

Use Case

Healthcare:
Virti's Immersive Learning for Healthcare Professionals

Virti leverages extended reality (XR) (Virti 2022), virtual reality (VR), and AI to provide immersive training for improved performance. During the COVID-19 pandemic, Virti released an AI-powered "virtual patient" to enhance remote clinical training for medical professionals and trainees across the NHS and hospitals in the US. The platform trained over 300 doctors at Cedars-Sinai Hospital in **high stakes** skills such as assessing patient symptoms and performing CPR while wearing protective clothing.

Consider this: The U.S. (IBIS World 2025) has over 23,000 driving schools, not to teach the mechanics of vehicles, but to prepare people to operate them **safely, confidently, and within limits.** In the same way, organizations must build structured AI learning ecosystems. These are not just technical programs, they are culture-shaping efforts that prepare every employee to steer with judgment, question with clarity, and lead with responsibility.

Lesson: Starting with their core domain skills, the intense training with robotic arms not only improved their tool literacy (How to use it) but allowed them to become fluent (Versatile in use) balancing safety and risk. Becoming confident and trusting their new tools allowed for "Scaling AI-Fluency" (Figure 9).

Executive Reflection

1. As AI becomes more accessible, are you investing in the organizational equivalent of "driving schools" to ensure responsible usage?
2. Have you mapped which roles require AI awareness versus AI fluency and tailored training accordingly?
3. Do your current training efforts focus only on tools, or do they also build judgment about interpreting and questioning AI outputs?
4. What mechanisms do you have to coach or retrain users who misuse or misunderstand AI applications?
5. Are you designing AI training to be dynamic and able to grow with new technologies, regulations, and ethical expectations?

Call to Action: Risk-Aware AI Training

Design the foundational model for an internal AI training program that treats employees not just as users, but as responsible "drivers" in your AI ecosystem.

Steps:

- Identify Common Risks: List potential risks associated with AI usage in your organization (e.g., data privacy concerns, algorithmic bias).
- Identify distinct user groups who engage with AI tools in your organization.
- Match each group to a training format: Awareness, Fluency, Expertise.
- Measure maturity: set one outcome metric per group (e.g., reduction in escalations, increase in successful prompt use, improved decision confidence).

Summary

AI is no longer confined to the technical elite. Its accessibility has expanded, much like how automobiles moved from luxury items to everyday tools. Yet, just as learning to drive requires education, practice, and an understanding of road safety, so too does navigating AI in the workplace.

Training-as-a-Service (TaaS) models provide organizations with the infrastructure to democratize AI fluency, while mitigating the risks of misuse. Responsible scaling of AI depends not just on distributing tools, but on fostering confidence, informed, and accountable users.

Lessons Learned

- AI adoption mirrors historical technology shifts where widespread value comes only after widespread understanding.
- Training at scale must move beyond basic how-to guides; it should embed judgment, ethics, and risk awareness.
- Not all users need to become data scientists; but all must become AI-literate.
- Teaching "how to drive" AI responsibly is not optional; it is **core to reducing organizational risk** and increasing AI value realization.

EDUCATE CONTINUOUSLY

Chapter 9: AI as a Strategic Capability

"Projects end. Capabilities evolve."

While many organizations launch AI with a high-stakes proof of concept, few succeed at converting those initial wins into long-term business value. Why? Because AI is still treated as a project, not a capability. Projects have deliverables, timelines, and budgets. Capabilities, by contrast, are embedded into the enterprise fabric; they are cross-functional, continuously funded, and outcome-focused.

This chapter explores how organizations can move beyond isolated "AI success stories" to build AI as a scalable, service-oriented capability, one that business teams can access, apply, and extend to support their goals. This is a key consideration when **aligning AI with business value.** A helpful analogy comes from agriculture: when soil loses its nutrients, known as soil leaching, chemical fixes only provide short term correction. For long term soil fertility global farming practices like crop rotation and intercropping are used to restore balance.

Business leaders must think like farmers, committed not just to short-term yield, but to the ongoing health and regenerative capacity of their AI landscape. If one use case does not yield immediate returns, it may still contribute to the richness of the data, processes, and infrastructure that enable future value generation.

Investing in strong foundations such as platform architecture, reusable processes, and institutional knowledge, is critical to developing AI capabilities that scale over time. These investments must be deliberate, vision-aligned, and tied to the organization's most strategic use cases.

The Big Problem

Too many organizations treat AI as a project to launch and not as a capability to grow. The term *Proof of Concept (POC) Purgatory* or the *POC graveyard* are branding that dissolve the innovative spirit of teams.

POC and prototyping focus on short-term wins, rapid experimentation, and isolated tools, hoping that success will scale itself. But scaling does not happen by accident. It happens through continuous, strategic planning that deliberately ties foundational investments, platforms, processes, and people, to evolving business needs.

AI that is not aligned to long-term vision becomes shelfware that is doomed. Worse, it becomes a credibility risk to the team, the tools and the potential of the vision it supported.

Real value to an AI-led vision in an organization comes from:

- Revisiting, reusing, and refining processes across use cases
- Building, sharing, and maturing knowledge foundations
- Investing in governance and learning loops, not just tooling

If we want AI to become part of the Enterprise's muscle, we need to stop planning around the next deployment and start reflecting and refining based on lessons learnt. **Projects end. Capabilities evolve.**

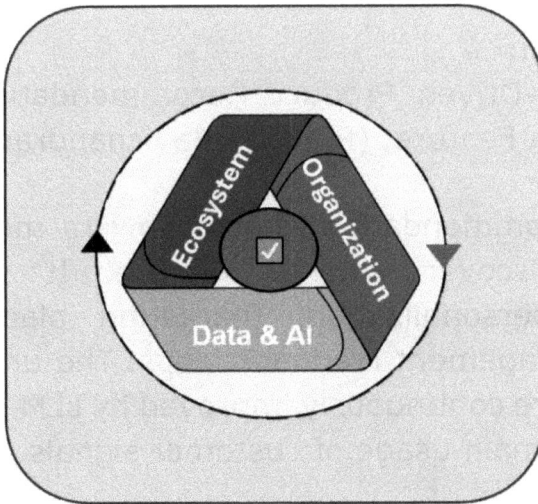

Figure 10: Continuous Strategic Planning

The development journey of AI workflows is seen as an outcome of continuous planning process.

Use Cases

Healthcare:

Anthem (Elevance Health) – AI for Clinical Workflow Automation (AWS 2022)

Anthem partnered with AWS to build an automated claims processing pipeline using Amazon Textract and AI-based OCR tools. This led to 80% automation in some workflows, freeing up clinicians and improving cycle times. Rather than building AI per use case, they created reusable services with modular APIs.

Lesson: Strategic AI capabilities require infrastructure **and** the playbook to support scalable reuse.

Internet Content:

Spotify – AI-Driven Product Recommendation as a Core Platform Feature. (Praveen Ravichandran 2024)

Spotify's recommendation engine powers more than just the 'Discover Weekly' feature. It supports homepage personalization, marketing placements, and user engagement feedback loops. The underlying AI systems are continuously improved by LLM research and cross-domain usage of customer signals.

Lesson: AI should be treated as platform capability, not just a feature. Strategic reuse of AI across the platform is enabled by shared ownership between product, content, engineering, and marketing teams.

Executive Reflection

1. Are AI efforts currently tied to timelines & budgets or to outcomes & service models?
2. How to convert the AI team to a capability team, from a delivery-only mode?
3. Do AI services have product owners or just sponsors for AI experiments?
4. How is reuse and adoption of AI tools being measured?

Call to Action: AI Capability Canvas

Create a one-page snapshot of how AI will evolve from isolated pilots to an enterprise service capability.

- Identify 2–3 AI solutions that have proven value in your org.
- Map the components they rely on (data, APIs, training workflows).
- Ask: How can these be modularized and offered as internal products?
- Define the internal customer segments (who benefits from this capability?).
- Set one service-level metric (uptime, latency, number of reuse cases, NPS).
- Identify one blocker to capability scaling (e.g., funding, ownership, architectural fit).

Summary

AI must evolve from an innovation silo to a repeatable business-enabling capability. Projects win headlines. Capabilities build competitive advantage. This requires not just models but infrastructure, incentives, service-level thinking, and team empowerment. This chapter serves as a transition point, linking human enablement and AI literacy (Chapter 8) to innovation at the edge (Chapter 10) and platform maturity (Chapter 11).

Lessons Learned

- AI tied only to use cases will struggle to scale.
- Strategic capabilities are modular, monitored, and co-owned.
- Capability thinking aligns AI with platform, process, and product innovation.
- Measuring adoption and reuse is key to realizing ROI across the organization.

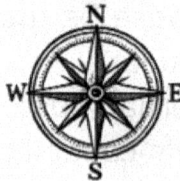

ANCHOR IN BUSINESS VALUE

Chapter 10: Innovation at the Edge

"The edge is where AI gets real."

Centralized AI strategies are important—but they are not where all innovation happens. In fact, some of the most impactful and adaptive AI applications emerge at the edges of the enterprise: marketing teams experimenting with GenAI for content creation, supply chain leaders using AI to reduce waste, or customer service teams refining chatbots based on real-time interactions.

The Industrial Revolution in Great Britain was not a sudden burst of advancement— it was the result of cumulative breakthroughs that were built up in increments and fed off one another. The invention of the cotton gin to separate sticky seeds from cotton fibers, or the shift from dim tallow to brighter coal gas street lighting, reshaped not just production methods, but entire cultural and economic outlooks. Labor skills of cotton pickers changed to mill jobs, and people stayed out later feeling more secure with brighter streetlights.

In the same way, AI innovation does not arrive at a single dramatic moment. It evolves through distributed experimentation and operational iteration. Progress can be subtle yet impactful—like UPS's famous "no left turn" logistics strategy to save fuel and time, or the introduction of car assembly lines moving car along the assembly line instead of people. Even the revolving door—originally introduced to reduce energy loss in buildings—is an example of how small innovations, once scaled, create meaningful energy savings impact.

The Big Problem

Innovative approaches using AI applications are feasible only if the AI infrastructure enables the flow of quality data or information through the ecosystem.

Figure 11: AI at the Edge

AI fluency and AI literacy influence the end-point developers, users, or consumers to explore incremental modifications to the process, use of insights delivered, or be creative with the applications.

While many AI strategies begin at the center, they rarely mature without experimentation at the edge. The challenge is autonomy with governance to ensure innovation aligns with enterprise goals.

This chapter explores how organizations foster innovation at the edge, ensure it aligns with enterprise goals, and balance autonomy with oversight. It also sets the stage for Chapter 11, where we examine how technology-as-a-service enables sustainable scaling and governance across distributed teams.

Use Cases

Consumer Products:
Unilever – Decentralized AI in Supply Chain and Marketing (Unilever 2025)

Unilever has implemented AI-driven customer connectivity models to enhance its supply chain operations. For instance, in a pilot with Walmart Mexico, product availability at the point of sale increased to 98%. This model is now being rolled out across 30 key customers globally, starting in the UK and US.

Additionally, Unilever's ice cream supply chain leverages AI and digital tools to respond to changing weather patterns, optimize inventory, reduce waste, and identify growth opportunities in a highly seasonal business, while staying aligned with central governance protocols.

Lesson: Edge innovation thrives when data infrastructure and governance enable safe experimentation.

Farm Equipment:

John Deere – Edge AI for Precision Farming (Wilson 2023)

Using AI-enabled sensors and autonomous tractors, John Deere puts decision-making closer to the field literally. Real-time data from soil and crop sensors allow for micro-level treatment of land. The 8R tractor, for example, uses six pairs of stereo cameras and AI to perceive its environment and navigate fields autonomously. This innovation addresses labor shortages and enhances **productivity** in agriculture.

These systems were not centrally designed but evolved in partnership with R&D and farmers.

Lesson: Innovation happens fastest when the people closest to the problem are part of the solution.

Food Services:
MOD Pizza – AI for Operations Innovation

MOD Pizza (SAP 2025), a fast casual restaurant piloted an AI-driven workforce optimization and predictive scheduling tool at select locations. Labor efficiency was assessed at limited high-volume stores, involving local managers and crews leads. AI-adoption culture was also tested based on team morale and customer experiences. They used,

- Edge experimentation collecting location-level inputs and buy-in.
- Provided governed autonomy by setting ethical guidelines from leadership and employers.
- Established a feedback loop from the stores to help broader rollout and learning.

Lesson: Empowering frontline managers with AI tools, paired with ethical guidelines, can lead to innovation in labor optimization without sacrificing culture or consistency.

Strategic Insights

Leaders drive edge innovation by creating the right conditions: granting access to tools, setting clear guardrails, and offering continuous support. As local teams are empowered with autonomy and flexibility, organizations can unlock meaningful business outcomes **within a well-governed framework**.

But a word of caution: **autonomy without alignment creates silos.** Innovation must be scaled with coordination, not chaos.

Executive Reflection

1. Are you creating space for innovation at the edges of your business?
2. Does your frontline team have access to safe, scalable AI tools, and autonomy to test ideas?
3. How do you track, share, or scale successful experiments at the edge?
4. Are you training local teams to think like "AI product managers" within their domains?

Call to Action: Audit the Edge

Choose a business unit or geography. Map where innovation is happening with or without central AI support.

- What AI tools or solutions are being used today?
- Who initiated these innovations?
- Are they supported by core data platforms or operating in silos?
- What lessons have emerged from this use case that could apply elsewhere?
- How could you better support or scale this kind of innovation?

Summary

Innovation at the edge is not an outlier. It is a strategic pattern. Organizations that win with AI give teams the tools, trust, and autonomy to solve problems in real time. They also create connective tissue across governance, platforms, and communities. This helps to scale those insights across the enterprise.

Lessons Learned

- Empowering the edge speeds up experimentation and relevance.
- Governance should enable and **not restrict** local creativity.
- Data access and modular platforms are key enablers of distributed innovation.
- Sharing success stories across business units builds institutional momentum for AI.

ORCHESTRATE, DO NOT COMMAND

Chapter 11: Building An AI Ecosystem

"AI does not live in isolation—it thrives in ecosystems."

Lego blocks offer a powerful metaphor for designing AI systems. Using the different Lego pieces strong and stable structures can be created. They may be pieces of varying size, length, color or even shape. The basic modularity and a standardized locking system allows for creativity and stability of structures.

The AI ecosystem is not just a stack of tools. It is a coordinated system of platforms, workflows, infrastructure, and people that together deliver AI at-scale. These components must align with business goals—not operate as isolated point solutions. Like a Lego structure, a healthy AI ecosystem should be **modular, reusable**, and **interconnected,** enabling flexibility without sacrificing structural integrity.

In contrast, Jenga towers can be seen as a stack of blocks which destabilize quickly as you proceed with the game- of removing the foundational layer at the bottom.

AI systems can collapse in a similar way. Especially when teams operate in silos, reuse is limited, or foundational investments like data governance and leadership alignment are missing.

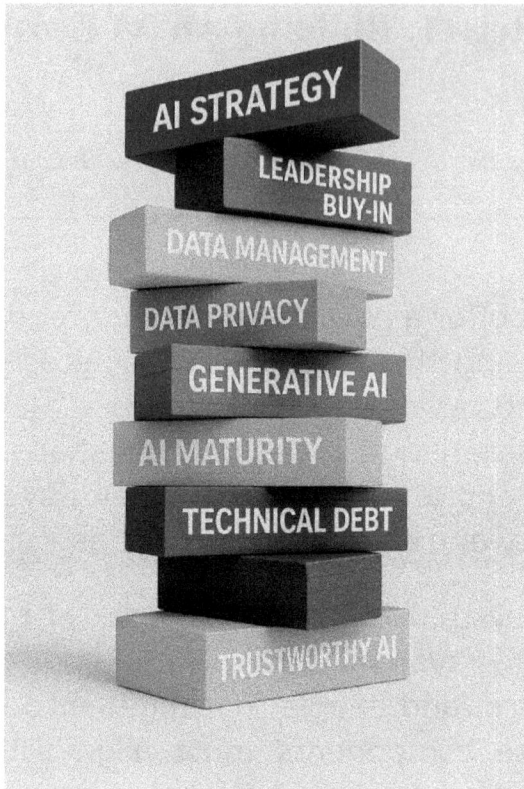

Figure 12: AI Jenga Tower Not Ecosystem

When you consider the popular AI approaches used, we need to sharpen our tech-fluency and learn about their specific needs. Both ML and GenAI architectures have unique needs: ML depends on structured pipelines and lifecycle orchestration, while GenAI systems require prompt management, Retrieval-Augmented Generation (RAG) (IBM Technology 2023), and tuning workflows. But they all **depend on the same structural integrity**: modularity, reuse, and shared components.

As we discussed in Chapter 9, treating AI as a strategic capability means designing for flexibility and evolution. Your systems must be able to support new use cases, accommodate emerging tools, and adapt to shifting priorities without breaking under the weight of their own complexity.

The Big Problem

Many organizations begin with successful AI pilots, prototypes, or POCs but struggle to scale. The common culprits?

- Fragmented tooling
- Siloed teams
- Lack of shared architecture or best practices

ML platforms often evolve from regression modeling workflows—but require intentional investment in **model reuse, lineage, and traceability**. GenAI tools, meanwhile, frequently proliferate without coordinated governance, leading to **redundancy, compliance risk, and spiraling costs**.

How should we think when building resilience and not rigidity into our ecosystem? The ability to flex, rebalance, and grow without collapsing under its own complexity.

To avoid building brittle AI structures that are not sustainable, organizations must ask the question:

Are we building for resilience or just assembling for a result?

Strategic Insight: Resilient AI Ecosystem

A resilient AI ecosystem is not rigid. It flexes, rebalances, and grows—**without collapsing under its own complexity**.

A well-designed AI ecosystem includes both general and specialized layers:

- **Core Platforms**: ML pipelines, model registries, LLM orchestration layers

- **Modularity:** APIs, containers, and services that allow flexibility and reuse

- **Shared Components**: Feature stores for ML, prompt libraries and vector databases for GenAI

- **Governance Overlays**: Policy enforcement, lineage, audit, and monitoring tools, performance and quality management

While ML ecosystems emphasize data labeling, model tuning, and scoring pipelines, GenAI ecosystems focus on prompt engineering, retrieval layers, and scalable inference endpoints. Both have their unique flows to generate outcomes and insights that feedback into updates of underlying models.

Use Cases

Online Merchandizing:
Wayfair's Mercury Platform (Alexander Hristov 2023) was designed to support scalable ML applications through programmatic feature definition, build, and maintenance. By building a robust feature library with 1000's of features (modular components), they enabled the reuse of maintainable features. Their platform was able to support 20+ ML applications using 100's of models driving online sales, distribution, pricing, and warehouse inventory management.

Lesson: Reusable infrastructure multiplies impact – this is realized from the investment in maintainable programmatic feature engineering library. It allowed scaling through multiple use cases leveraging the built features.

Wealth Management:
Morgan Stanley – GenAI + RAG for Wealth Management

Morgan Stanley (OpenAI 2025) developed an internal AI assistant powered by OpenAI's GPT models and a proprietary retrieval-augmented generation system. This tool helps financial advisors query internal knowledge, supported by a strong evaluation framework to ensure reliability. Today, over 98% of advisor teams actively use *AI@MorganStanley*

Assistant to enhance their productivity and client interactions.

Lesson: Building trust for scale. Creating reliable and faster information access through AI assistant preserves the balance in a personal and value deepening client relationships while scaling.

Software Application:
Zoom – GenAI Summarization Across Ecosystem Layers

Zoom (Zoom Blog 2024) introduced AI companion tools for meeting summarizations, chat and productivity enhancements by integrating LLM APIs and prompt workflows into their collaboration platform. The AI Companion empowers individuals by helping them be more productive, connect and collaborate with teammates, and improve their skills by providing the services of a digital assistant.

Lesson: Seamless integration of shared components drives adoption through better accessibility and reducing customer friction.

Executive Reflection

1. Are your AI tools designed for interoperability across ML and GenAI workflows?
2. Do you have reusable infrastructure components like prompt libraries or feature stores?
3. Think about infrastructure design with auditability and policy enforcement built in? E.g., Data quality and AI risk mitigation.
4. Are parts of your current AI landscape redundant, underused, or incompatible?

Call To Action: Map AI Ecosystem

Fill in the table below for your organization's AI systems.

Use this to assess whether each layer supports ML, GenAI, or both—and identify gaps in modularity and reuse.

A few examples of what system components you should be asking questions about are provided.

Questions about the important system components that should be addressed may include the components within these layers. A sample is provided on the table below.

Table 3: Ecosystem Layers- ML vs. GenAI

Layer	System Examples	ML Role	GenAI Role
Data Ingestion	Kafka, APIs, Snowflake streams	Feature feeds for models	Prompt data or context inputs
Storage	Data lakes, vector databases	Training/ validation data	RAG source corpora
Model Serving	SageMaker, Vertex AI, Azure ML	Model endpoints for scoring	LLM inference endpoints
Governance	Data catalogs, policy engines, quality	Access, drift monitoring	Prompt/LLM auditing and monitoring

Summary

Scalable AI doesn't come from standalone tools. It comes from connected ecosystems.

While machine learning and generative AI require different infrastructure elements, pipelines vs. prompts, models vs. retrieval layers, they both demand standardization, governance, and modular design to operate at scale.

Building your AI ecosystem is not about choosing the flashiest platform. It is about designing a foundation that can **evolve with innovation, reduce duplication**, and **lower the cost of change**.

The most successful organizations invest in architecture, not just applications.

Lessons Learned

- Ecosystems scale value, not just tools. AI power comes from a connected grid that supports reuse, extensions and enterprise accessibility.

- Modularity multiplies reuse. Data pipelines, feature/prompt stores, and observability tools are critical components that can be made modular

- Cross-layer integration unlocks adoption-coordinating not just models and data, but also prompts, APIs, user interfaces, and monitoring tools.

- ML and GenAI share some common infrastructural needs. But their strategic use cases are unique and demand distinctive infrastructure strategy.

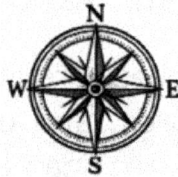

EMBED FEEDBACK LOOPS

Chapter 12: Tech-as-a-Service: The AI Backbone

"AI maturity does not mean building more. It means enabling more."

In many ways, the evolution of the U.S. energy grid offers a powerful analogy for how AI infrastructure must evolve. Historically, electric utilities operated as vertically integrated monopolies owning everything from generation to distribution. While effective in a centralized world, this model eventually stifled flexibility, competition, and innovation. With the deregulation of the energy sector in the 1970s and 1990s, the grid became more modular and dynamic, enabling new players to generate and distribute power across interconnected systems.

Today, even households can produce energy through rooftop solar, feeding into a more resilient, distributed grid. But the 2021 Texas power crisis (Wikipedia 2025) is a sobering reminder of what happens in the absence of interconnection: isolated systems become limited to a fixed capacity, prone to failure, unable to adapt in times of distress or offer backup energy services if their grid is down. Texas power customers had to wait out a whole week to get power again. The grid could not borrow power from other companies as they had chosen to be independent. They were not connected to neighboring energy grids.

AI infrastructure faces a similar inflection point. Building isolated models and pipelines that cannot tap into shared data sources, model registries, or monitoring frameworks leads to duplication, blind spots, and organizational fragility. With scaling AI in mind, technology leaders should engage with partners across the organization, build a catalog of potential AI use cases and use that to build **core infrastructure** systems that can provide a reusable architecture design across the organization i.e., **a modular intelligent grid.**

Organizations should be focused on their core competencies, product and service innovation, not reinventing complex infrastructure. Internal technology teams built, and customized monolithic systems tightly coupled to business. Today they need to become **designers of service-based AI** platforms: helping orchestrate the infrastructure that allows experimentation, reuse, and scaled innovation. With technology-as-a-Service (TaaS), internal teams can focus on effective utilization, test domain-specific innovation, and scale with confidence.

While TaaS unlocks flexibility there are some challenges organizations must address as well:

- Integration challenges across legacy systems

- Security concerns with external vendors
- Misaligned SLAs or vendor lock-in risks

To scale AI responsibly, we need the equivalent of a robust, interconnected grid: modular platforms that deliver intelligence as a service, with visibility, flexibility, and shared value across the enterprise.

The Big Problem

In the past, internal technology teams were architects of bespoke systems because core intelligence of a business was embedded in proprietary systems. But today, the landscape has shifted. Modular, cloud-native, and open-source tools have democratized access to AI components, fundamentally changing the role of internal tech teams.

How do you operationalize intelligence without reinventing the wheel?

This is where Technology-as-a-Service (TaaS) enters on the maturity roadmap. It offers a path to scalable, governed, and reusable AI services delivered across the enterprise.

AI maturity doesn't mean building more. It means enabling more.

The real challenge now is operationalizing intelligence with modularity, oversight, and agility, building an AI platform that does not just support one solution, but accelerates everyone.

Can business trust the shift to this new role?

The figure 'Scaling AI Technology' illustrates how the role of technology teams is shifting. From infrastructure owners to orchestrators of scalable, modular AI capabilities that others in the business can consume on demand.

Today many organizations still approach AI from a "tech stack" mindset. They focus on tools but overlook trust boundaries required for adoption. In a TaaS model, success depends not just on technical delivery, but on cultural readiness, transparency, and learning.

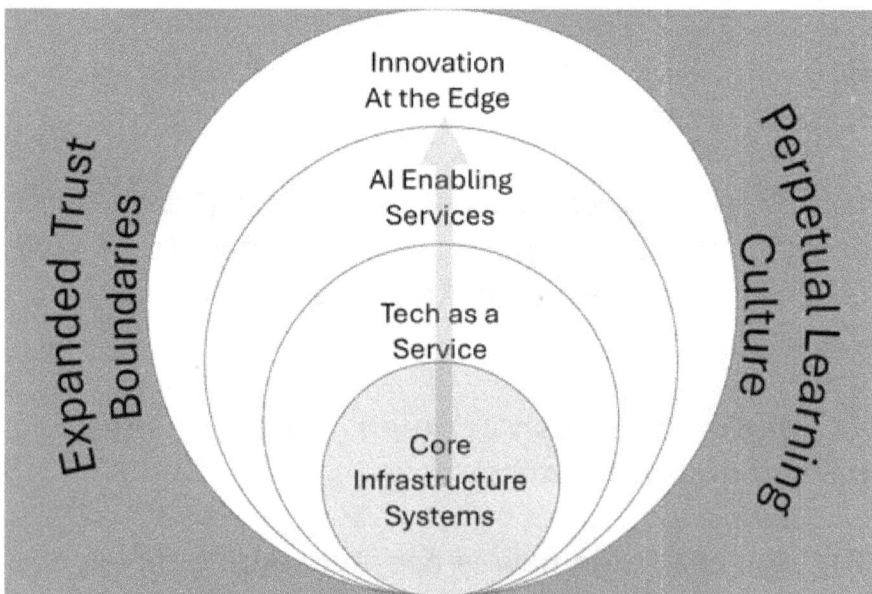

Innovation
At the Edge

AI Enabling
Services

Tech as a
Service

Core
Infrastructure
Systems

Expanded Trust
Boundaries

Perpetual Learning
Culture

Figure 13: Scaling AI Technology

Leaders who embed TaaS as both a platform **and a shared service culture** are the ones who scale AI responsibly—and repeatedly.

Use Cases

Airlines:
Lufthansa Systems – AI-Powered Crew Management as a Cloud Service

Lufthansa (Lufthansa Systems 2024) developed an AI-powered platform to predict crew disruptions and optimize scheduling across its airline operations. Rather than embedding AI into a single workflow, they exposed the platform as a cloud-based internal service that was usable by both Lufthansa teams and partner airlines.

Lesson: Modularity and service delivery enable scalable, cross-functional AI capabilities.

Media:
Netflix – Internal AI Infrastructure as a Self-Service Platform

Netflix democratizes AI through internal platforms like Metaflow and Polynote (Chemitiganti 2025), allowing engineers and data scientists to rapidly build, train, and deploy models. These tools abstract the infrastructure complexity and integrate with governance, version control, and logging.

Lesson: Self-service tooling enables experimentation without chaos supported by reusability, standardization, and observability of the processes.

Strategic Insight: Shared AI Technology

AI becomes a shared enterprise capability when infrastructure is modular, standards are clear, and teams are empowered to build on a common foundation.

Service-based design turns internal tools into accelerators fueling responsible experimentation and cross-functional reuse.

Executive Reflection

As your organization advances in AI maturity, ask:

1. Are you investing in infrastructure and building a culture that knows how to use it?
2. What does "enablement" mean for business users, not just data teams? Define it!
3. How do you ensure governance doesn't slow down experimentation but scales with it?
4. Are the platforms designed for AI services for reuse, governed for scale, and trusted by business?

Call To Action: Match TaaS with AI Path

Identify and evaluate the modularity and service readiness of your AI stack for 3–5 recurring AI use cases or models in your organization. For each, ask:

- Is it centrally managed or domain-owned?
- Can it be replaced by a reusable internal service?
- Does it integrate into broader observability/governance platforms?
- Define what it would take to make your AI stack more modular, measurable, and service-enabled.

Summary

AI maturity is not about building more. It is about enabling more. Scaling AI requires a shift from custom tools to modular, service-based infrastructure. That shift requires a mindset change. Culture is the true enabler.

Organizations that succeed do not just optimize their platform, they create in shared standards, invest in training, and build feedback loops that foster trust between builders and users. When tech teams become service enablers, innovation scales, without compromising governance or agility.

Lessons Learned

- Infrastructure is not enough, AI services must be designed for reusability, governance, and adaptability
- Modularity enables scale, but culture sustains it.
- Tech teams must shift roles from builders to enablers
- Standardization accelerates experimentation

EDUCATE CONTINUOSLY

Chapter 13: Strategic Choices: Build, Buy, or Borrow AI

"In AI, the wrong investment is not just a sunk cost—it is a missed opportunity."

As AI adoption matures, leaders face a recurring question: **Should we build this in-house, buy from a vendor, or borrow through partnerships and open platforms?** These are not just technical decisions, they are strategic bets that shape talent needs, time-to-value, differentiation, and risk exposure.

The right starting point is clarity of the business goals. Leadership must assess **the anticipated value** of AI initiatives. An **economic value analysis** of the data–AI–information ecosystem reveals the true cost and potential returns. With that understanding, the timeline becomes the next decision lever where urgency and AI readiness may justify buying or borrowing instead of building.

AI readiness assessment becomes a pre-required first step in the decisioning process. Nimble organizations, especially SMBs and startups, can use emerging technologies to leapfrog incumbents, unlocking new revenue streams or carving out a competitive niche. In contrast, larger enterprises still in the middle of digital transformation may lack the agility or internal alignment to support a successful "AI build" approach in the near term. Especially if some of the AI needs were not part of the ongoing transformation.

The current AI applications landscape is rich with options. At the same time, it can feel overwhelming and opaque. Compatibility questions, integration hurdles, or misaligned promises often surface, especially when organizational AI maturity is low. In such cases, early and fast experimentation through value-focused proofs of concept may be the best approach. Leaders must weigh speed, differentiation, and trust boundaries, not just tools.

Discussions in Chapter 9 and 12 connect AI platform maturity to sourcing decisions in this chapter. Sourcing decisions should be considered with capability maturity, AI literacy, and presence of AI platform foundations in mind. The right choice, whether to build, buy, or borrow, will ultimately depend on your business goals and risk appetite for financial, market, and operational risks.

The Big Problem

Most organizations make decisions on AI sourcing based on urgency, trend, vendor recommendations, or budgetary constraints. Compatibility with strategic vision, insights from end user teams, and business use cases, are often overlooked or **overshadowed**. Long-term value and capability alignments and AI-readiness are fleetingly considered.

The result: Technical assets that do not mature into strategic capabilities. A mature organization should evaluate when to own, when to accelerate and when to partner based on matching the organization's trajectory with common patterns shown below.

Strategic Insight: AI Investment Choices

Sourcing AI capabilities is not just a technical choice it is a leadership decision.

For many small and mid-sized businesses, the availability of in-house AI teams may be limited. As technology evolves rapidly, borrowing **off-the shelf tools**, such as API's, open-source models, pre-trained domain specific GenAI models, can offer **low-risk entry point**. This approach to AI adoption also provides an opportunity to experiment, build internal fluency, and assess alignment with business needs. You are not just borrowing technical capability but also buying time to scale your internal capabilities.

Today's sourcing decision shapes tomorrow's platform maturity. You are not just borrowing technology—you are borrowing time to build trust, skill, and strategic alignment.

In the table 'Build, Buy, or Borrow- Making Sense', a basic assessment guidance is provided. While this may not be the complete list, they represent key factors in the leadership decision that you will face.

Table 4: Build, Buy, or Borrow – Making Sense

Mode	When it Makes Sense	Risks or Watchouts
Build	When AI is core to your product or differentiator	Long lead times, talent dependencies
Buy	When speed and scale are critical	Vendor lock-in, generic capabilities
Borrow	When open-source or partnerships offer strategic leverage	Integration burden, compliance variability

Use Cases

Banking:
Capital One – Build for Core Differentiation

Capital One (Bean 2024) built its internal ML platform, "Model Factory", to standardize AI workflows across business units. This decision was aligned with AI's strategic role in fraud detection and customer personalization, which was core to their long-term competitiveness.

Lesson: When AI is business-critical, owning the stack ensures control, governance, and long-term adaptability.

Pharma:
Pfizer – Buy and Partner for Speed (Pfizer 2022)

Amid the urgency of COVID-19 vaccine development, Pfizer leveraged cloud providers like AWS and Azure ML and partnered with algorithm developers to accelerate large-scale simulations and discovery efforts.

Lesson: When time-to-value is paramount, buying and borrowing can speed up delivery without compromising quality.

Health Services:
Sempre Health – Borrow Expert Acceleration Program

Sempre Health (Hugging Face 2022) a mid-sized health technology company focused on patient engagement, partnered with Hugging Face through its *Expert Acceleration Program* to implement natural language processing (NLP) capabilities. While the team had foundational skills in ML and NLP, they lacked the time and infrastructure to build a robust pipeline from scratch.

They **borrowed pre-trained models** and leveraged Hugging Face's guidance to rapidly integrate AI into their messaging system. As a result, nearly *20% of patient messages were handled automatically*, improving responsiveness without additional headcount.

Lesson: Strategic borrowing accelerates impact, especially when paired with expert support. For mid-sized firms, open-source and API ecosystems offer a fast track to learning and value realization.

Executive Reflection

1. **Strategic Fit:** Which AI capabilities are core to your competitive advantage?
2. **Time-to-Value:** Where is speed-to-market more valuable than customization?
3. **Vendor Strategy:** How do you evaluate and mitigate vendor dependency or data lock-in?
4. **Organizational learning**: Are you building repeatable internal learning, or just technical assets?

Call to Action: "Buy-Build-Borrow" Decision

Select 3 current or upcoming AI initiatives. For each, evaluate across 4 dimensions:

1. Strategic importance (Core vs. Supporting)
2. Time sensitivity (Now vs. Later)
3. Data control required (High vs. Low)
4. Talent readiness (Available vs. Need to hire)

- Use simple rubric to assess the fit of the individual decisions against your strategic goals.

AI Capability Sourcing Matrix

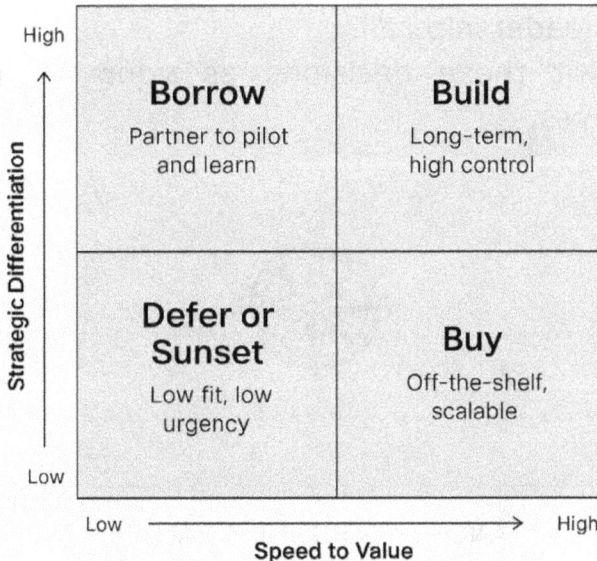

Figure 14: AI Investment Decisions

Summary

There is no one-size-fits-all answer to AI capability sourcing. Strategic clarity, not technical bias, should drive your decision. Whether you build, buy, or borrow, the real investment is in how you scale, learn from that decision, and mature the AI ecosystems to deliver business value.

Lessons Learned

- Build when AI is your IP. Buy when it accelerates value. Borrow when you need flexibility.
- Overbuilding creates debt; overbuying creates lock-in. Balance is key.
- Capability sourcing is not a technical decision; it is a leadership call.
- Revisit these decisions as your AI maturity evolves.

ANCHOR IN BUSINESS VALUE

Chapter 14: Responsible AI by Design

"If your people are not ready for AI, your business is not either."

As AI becomes more embedded into products, decisions, and customer experiences, organizations must ensure its responsible use from the outset and not bolted on, after deployment. Just as cybersecurity evolved from an afterthought to core design principles and now is embedded into all system designs.

Let us play out a familiar comic scene: A leader calls for a volunteer from the single row of cadets, and everyone steps back, leaving one unassuming person stranded in front. Sound familiar? Will you be the leader to step forward or step back? Will you wait for someone to take ownership of the task or intentionally choose to lead?

AI risk mitigation is not a one resource or a one leader job. (The above scene should not playout!)

It requires **collective accountability**. From the frontline staff to executive leadership. Unlike cybersecurity and compliance, which require frequent reminders through mandatory training or simulated drills, Responsible AI must prevail across everyday decisions, especially as GenAI tools become personal and professional defaults.

That's why we need a shift: from reactive enforcement to a proactive design. Enter the **RADAR approach**: a pragmatic framework that helps organizations operationalize Responsible AI at-scale. It promotes **organizational clarity and individual accountability**, enabling a shared understanding of what ethical AI looks like in your specific context.

Whether you are defining fairness thresholds or managing trade-offs between automation and oversight, your people must be equipped with a **moral compass** they can apply consistently: not a checklist they apply selectively.

The Big Problem

Responsible AI is still an afterthought for most organizations. It is relegated to compliance checks after a model is built, deployed and embedded into workflows. Since March 2022, the world has witnessed a wave of AI-related harms: hallucinations, biased judgements, discrimination, data misuse and real human consequences. This damage has resulted from the way AI was used or interpreted. The damage is often irreversible.

Treating Responsible AI as a post-deployment checklist is simply too little, too late. The cost of inaction includes:

- Regulatory fines and noncompliance

- Biased or unfair outcomes
- Poor transparency in decision-making
- Erosion of customer trust and employee morale

Instead, AI must be designed with a **human-centric framework** from the start, one that includes fairness, transparency, accountability, and safety as core principles of development. Retroactive patches applied after launch cannot recover easily from the incurred cost of inaction.

Key questions leadership should be asking:

- What compliance standards should be applied for readiness?
- Have checks for bias and fairness been conducted?
- Is the data-to-decision lineage traceable and explainable and understood by the business?
- Is inclusivity part of the design or is the focus on efficiency alone?

At the organizational level, this chapter explores how to embed fairness, transparency, accountability, and safety into the design and governance of AI systems, so they scale not just fast, but scale right to continue delivering business value.

Use Cases

Technology:
Microsoft – Responsible AI Standard Framework

Microsoft (Microsoft 2025) developed a **Responsible AI Standard**, complete with internal toolkits, checklists and review processes for fairness, reliability, inclusiveness, and transparency. Ethics check-ins and escalation pathways are integrated into their product development lifecycle through

Lesson: Embedding responsible design requires structured tools, cross-functional processes, and leadership sponsorship.

Social Media:
Pinterest – Inclusive AI Through Representative Training Data

Pinterest (Pinterest 2023) redesigned its image search AI to better reflect diverse body types and skin tones by curating inclusive datasets and publishing their methodology Pinterest encouraged others, industry-wide to focus on algorithmic equity lapses.

Lesson: Bias mitigation is not just technical; it is a design principle that begins with data stewardship and inclusivity.

The "coded gaze" is a term coined by Joy Buolamwini (Buolamwini 2024) reminds us that **AI systems reflect the perspectives, and the blind spots, of their creators**. This means that facial recognition code in AI systems can be biased towards certain groups or demographics due to the limited scope of the developers in training for diverse ethnic skin tones. Joy's live demonstration, using facemasks, set off deeper evaluation of the AI code bias.

Similarly, profiling biases of training data can lead to unfair and unethical decisions being delivered by AI applications that impact individual customers and communities alike.

Executive Reflection

1. Have you defined what 'Responsible AI' means in your organizational context?
2. Does your AI team include legal, risk, and ethics expertise at the design phase?
3. Are you continuously monitoring models for bias, drift, and unintended outcomes?
4. Have you built escalation paths for issues that emerge post-deployment?

Call to Action: Responsible AI Checklist

Choose an existing or planned AI use case. Assess it using the following design checkpoints:

1. **Fairness:** Have you audited for bias in data or outcomes?

2. **Explainability:** Can decision-making be communicated clearly to users and regulators?

3. **Safety & Security:** Are you protected against misuse, model poisoning, or adversarial attacks?

4. **Accountability:** Who owns the AI's behavior post-deployment?

5. **User Impact:** Have you considered the downstream consequences on humans, communities, or social trust?

6. **Professional responsibility** through RADAR

Summary

Responsible AI must be designed in, not layered on. Organizations that embed fairness, transparency, and accountability into their AI lifecycle will build trust, avoid regulatory and reputational risk, and create systems that benefit more people, more sustainably.

Lessons Learned

- Responsible AI is not a standalone team; it is a cross-functional commitment.
- Tools, templates, and rituals like ethics reviews normalize responsible practice.

RADAR Framework for Responsible AI

The RADAR© framework (Sarathy 2024) offers a structured approach for embedding responsible AI practices into daily decision-making at both individual and organizational levels. It encourages teams to proactively address ethics, accountability, and transparency throughout the AI lifecycle.

Table 5: Explaining RADAR Actions

STEP	DESCRIPTION
READ	Stay informed about the AI systems in your environment and understand their purpose, scope, and potential risks.
ASK	Raise questions about fairness, accountability, and ethical impact during the design and deployment of AI systems.
DOCUMENT	Keep a clear and auditable trail of model design, decisions, datasets, and assumptions.
AWARE	Recognize when harm, bias, or drift may have occurred—and escalate concerns.
REPORT	Implement clear, accessible channels to surface and respond to ethical or operational issues in AI use.

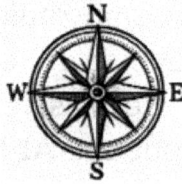

GOVERN FOR TRUST, NOT CONTROL

Chapter 15: The AI-Enabled Enterprise

"It is not just about having AI. It is about being changed by it."

The diagram below illustrates how data, technology, and AI fluency intersect to define modern AI-enabled leadership.

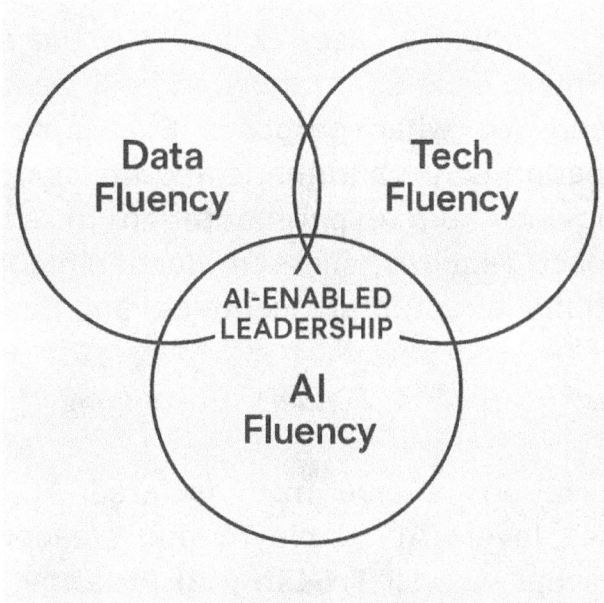

Figure 15: Tri-Lingual Fluency Diagram

Think of AI adoption like switching from a compass to a GPS. A compass offers direction: it is simple, static, and reactive. A GPS, by contrast, is dynamic: it recalculates in real time based on traffic, construction, and unexpected detours. An AI-enabled enterprise operates like a GPS: It does not just execute plans; it adapts continuously, informed by signals across data, people, and processes.

This adaptability becomes critical when operating in uncertainty, with messy data, rare edge cases, and with business policies and markets constantly in flux. Orchestrating effective AI solutions in such conditions can overwhelm the capacity of siloed teams.

Finding the right use cases is only half the equation. Leaders must understand how AI will be used, by whom, and for what purpose. Enterprise-wide AI transformation is not automatic and needs more than pilots. Moving from experimentation to enterprise-wide impact requires shifts in leadership mindset, organizational structures, incentives, and fluency.

Tri-Lingual Fluency: AI Leadership Language

As organizations evolve from isolated AI pilots to Enterprise level AI deployments, leaders must cultivate what we call **Tri-Lingual Fluency.** Leaders should have a working knowledge across data, technology, and AI capabilities.

Fluency is not about establishing domain expertise. Instead it is the leadership skill of translating across the disciplines of facilitation, communication, and cross-team collaboration. The fluent leader is a **translator and orchestrator** and can:

- Frame opportunities grounded in data reality
- Design solutions that fit the platform constraints
- Anticipate outcomes for the AI methods adopted

AI leadership is increasingly about bridging cultural and technical divides. Tri-Lingual fluency allows leaders to integrate AI into how people work: across teams, partners, and customers. The three foundational domains are:

- **Data-aware:** Understanding the quality, lifecycle, and readiness of data
- **Tech-aware:** Recognizing capabilities and constraints of platforms and architectures
- **AI-aware**: Distinguishing between automation, augmentation, and autonomy

An **AI-enabled enterprise** is not just about using AI. It is one **where AI shapes how the enterprise strategizes, reacts, and evolves** within their industry. As organizations cultivate a culture of AI literacy and alignment, teams will use AI intentionally: to solve problems, unlock innovations, and deliver measurable outcomes.

Three Shifts That Anchor AI-Driven Leadership

The journey towards becoming AI-enabled is not linear in time and effort. It requires coordinated shifts in mindset, engagement models, and an understanding of the purpose of AI across the enterprise.

These shifts do not replace leadership but reshape it.

Leaders with some degree of fluency across data, tech, and AI develop a system-level lens that allows them to react to evolving challenges by shifting their leadership styles.

> *"61% of data and analytics leaders involved in generative AI planning say that educating leadership is one of their primary responsibilities."*
>
> *- Ehtisham Zaidi, VP Analyst, Gartner*

Following the ideas from Ehtisham's talk Gartner (Alexis Wierenga 2024), your leadership compass must anchor to the following three shifts.

1. Mindset Shift
Leaders must move beyond command-and-control. Today's AI leader acts as an orchestrator, enabling empowered, cross-functional teams to surface, test, and scale ideas.

2. Engagement Shift

AI doesn't live in one team. It requires a culture of transparency, collaboration, and experimentation so that the outcomes are shaped not by isolated contributors but by connected responsibilities.

3. Purpose Shift

AI shouldn't be confined to POCs or end-of-process automation. Leaders must ensure that AI is embedded across the value chain, from operations to insight generation to innovation.

With these shifts a leader can assess the tactical steps needed to enable AI ecosystems and align them to scale sustainably. As fluency and trust deepen across the organization, AI adoption will accelerate through intentional and focused adoption for outcome-driven transformation.

Use Cases

Banking:
DBS Bank – Enterprise AI Transformation

DBS (McKinsey Blog 2025) adopted AI not just for customer insights, but to reshape how decisions were made across the business. AI tools were embedded in internal HR, finance, and operations functions, supported by a centralized platform team.

Lesson: A successful AI strategy is not just about being digitally successful; it has deep cultural requirements.

eCommerce & Personal Styling:
Stitch Fix – AI Integrated into Operating Model

Stitch Fix (Stitch Fix 2025) does not just use AI to recommend fashion. They used AI to co-manage inventory, design new items, and personalize the end-of-end customer experience. AI is treated as both a creative and operational partner.

Lesson: AI is not a tool. It is a collaborator built into the company's DNA.

Executive Reflection

1. Are you designing an ecosystem that responds to AI insights, or are you still expecting AI to fit into existing structures?

2. What learnings can redefine your leadership accountability around tri-lingual fluency?

3. What new roles, skills, and work practices can enable your teams to develop AI fluency?

4. Are you measuring AI success in terms of business value or just technical metrics?

Call to Action: Start AI-Enabled Leadership

Choose one core business function (e.g., marketing, operations, finance).

- Identify where AI is currently used: explicitly or implicitly.

- Define what decisions are still made without AI insights.

- Brainstorm how AI could augment, automate, or advise those decisions.

- Evaluate what structural or leadership changes would be needed to support that shift.

Summary

Becoming an AI-enabled enterprise is not about having the best tools, it is about rethinking how work happens. AI doesn't just automate processes; it reshapes roles, timelines, expectations, and learning cycles. Organizations that thrive will be those that redesign themselves to learn and adapt to AI and not just using them as tools.

Lessons Learned

- AI integration is cultural before it is technical.
- Leaders must evolve from decision-makers to sense-makers.
- Organizational agility, not just technical capability, defines enterprise AI maturity.
- AI maturity is measured by value realized, not pilots run.

TRI-LINGUAL FLUENCY

Chapter 16: AI Impact and Value

"You cannot scale what you cannot measure—and you cannot measure what you do not define."

AI promises transformation. But that transformation cannot be claimed. It must be demonstrated. We need to realize that transformation hinges on how we define, track, and act on success. Traditional return-on-investment (ROI) measures struggle to capture the dynamic, distributed, and cross-functional value of AI. We need a **new definition of success**.

To truly measure AI's impact, leaders must look beyond algorithmic accuracy or model performance and instead focus on business value creation, decision enhancement, and adaptability. Traditional ROI models struggle to account for AI's distributed, dynamic, and often indirect impact across workflows, teams, and customer experiences.

The deeper question is: **what did the AI system make possible that would not have happened otherwise?**

- Decisions made faster
- Opportunities surfaced earlier
- Risks mitigated more consistently
- Customers served more meaningfully

Defining the Business Value of AI

There needs to be a shift from **cost accounting to value creation accounting.** Business value refers to measurable outcomes that align with strategic goals. These may include:

- Revenue growth or protection
- Cost reduction or efficiency gains
- Risk mitigation or compliance assurance
- Customer experience and loyalty improvements
- Enablement of innovation or faster time-to-market

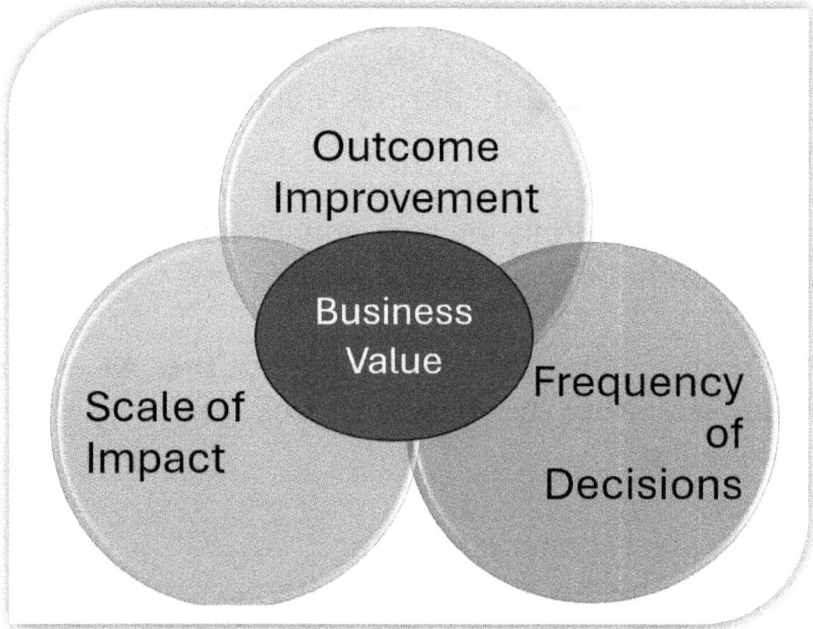

Figure 16: AI Business Value Determinants

Business value can be conceptually represented as:

**Business Value =
(Outcome Improvement × Scale of Impact ×
Frequency of Decision)**

AI enhances value not by doing new things, but by doing the right things faster, better, and more often.

Measuring Return on Investment (ROI)

**Traditional ROI =
(Financial Benefit – Cost of Investment) / Cost
of Investment**

For AI, this breaks down into:

Costs: Data acquisition and prep, modeling, deployment, monitoring, change management

Benefits: Reduced decision time, reduced errors, improved forecasts, personalized offers, proactive compliance

The difficulty is that most of AI's value is indirect or distributed across workflows and teams. That is where AI fluency and better impact mapping come in.

Framework – From Data to Business Impact

AI initiatives do not fail because of a lack of enthusiasm. They fail because impact is not measured at the level where decisions are made.

To translate AI activity into business value, we must examine the interacting layers of AI decision design: from the data foundations and technical performance to operational usage, business contribution, and long-term strategic alignment.

In the table below, metrics associated with the 5 key AI layers are illustrated with examples of metrics and some tactical discovery questions that one should ask.

Table 6: Aligning Metrics to Business Impact

AI Layer	Key Metric Types	Notes
Data Readiness	Quality scores, availability, latency	Do we have the data we need? Is it usable at speed?
Model Performance	Accuracy, recall, F1-score, bias	Traditional AI/ML KPIs (internal facing)
Operational Use	Time to deploy, adoption rate, query volume	Are people using it? How fast is it improving processes?
Business Value	Revenue per use, cost saved, risk avoided	Link outcomes to KPIs leaders care about
Strategic Fit	Contribution to goals, cross-team reuse	Is it aligned with business strategy and scaling potential?

As we discussed in Chapter 4, not all data is created equal. Some data drives front-line operational wins, while other data support strategic signals or experimentation. Similarly, not all metrics serve the same stakeholders.

This framework encourages leaders to assign ownership of metrics at each layer by asking teams to define what they are responsible for influencing. Doing so creates a culture of aligned accountability, where teams are not only tracking performance, but also seeing how their work connects to business impact.

By layering metrics in this way, you can:
- Clarify where friction or gaps exist in the AI lifecycle
- Connect technical metrics (e.g., latency, F1 score) with operational ones (e.g., adoption rate, query volume)
- Link platform investments and tool performance to visible business outcomes
- Anchor measurement in strategic contribution, not just activity tracking

Algorithmic vs. Business Metrics

While technical teams focus on algorithmic metrics, like precision, recall, or inference time, they alone do not signal business success.

Table 7: Aligning AI Metrics to Business Outcomes

Algorithmic Metrics	Business Metrics
Precision, Recall, AUC	ROI, Margin Growth, Conversion Rate
Model Training Time	Time to Value
Model Accuracy	Cost per Insight
Latency, Throughput	Decision Cycle Time

What matters at the executive level is **what changes** because of that model:
- Faster time to value,
- lower cost per insight, or
- improved conversion, retention and compliance.

The table above identifies a few ways to translate algorithmic metrics to business metrics.

To create enterprise-wide traction, we need to make these metrics interoperable. The ability to trace how improvements in model performance (e.g., faster inference or better accuracy) affect strategic indicators (e.g., faster decisions, higher ROI) is what turns technical wins into enterprise capability.

Insight: If AI doesn't influence decisions or delivers no measurable enterprise value then **do not use it**.

The AI Impact Equation

Too often, the impact of AI is not articulated and needs to be made visible using the three capability levers.

AI Impact = Data Maturity × Tech Enablement × Applied Use Case Fluency

Tri-Lingual Fluency (Data + Tech + AI/Business) guides the context of AI value to measure success:

- Do we have the right data?
- Are the platforms ready?
- Are the people applying it to real decisions?
- When these elements align, impact becomes visible and measurable.

Executive Reflection

1. Are you measuring what matters **or just** what is easy to measure?
2. Can you connect model outputs to business KPIs?
3. What percentage of deployed AI solutions are actively used at-scale?
4. How well do AI metrics support enterprise strategy and OKRs?

Call to Action: Focus on AI Value Chain

Choose one active or recent AI project. Then ask:
- What was the original goal? What KPI did it support?
- What technical metrics were used to assess models?
- How were business workflows affected?
- What was the realized impact (if any)?
- Where did the measurement stop? And why?

Summary

AI success is not just about models. It is about how AI consistently creates measurable business value. If teams cannot articulate the value, or track the impact, and communicate the value clearly, then AI programs will not be able to scale with confidence.

Lessons Learned

- AI success is defined by decision value, not technical accuracy.
- Measurement should connect input, processes, and outcomes.
- Business fluency must be built into every AI conversation.
- If no one owns the measurement, no one owns the value.

MEASURE WHAT MATTERS

Notes:

Chapter 17: Leading Forward – The AI Leadership Playbook

"AI leadership is not about knowing all the answers. It is about building systems that learn with you."

Beyond the Last Chapter

AI maturity is not a destination. It is a discipline grounded in curiosity, adaptation and shared learning. Today, leaders are being asked to approve models or invest in platforms and to champion systems of learning across data, people, and purpose evolve together.

Think of AI leadership like conducting an orchestra. The conductor does not play every instrument, but they set the tempo, unify the rhythm, and bring out the potential of every section. They do not dictate each note but ensure harmony, transitions, and momentum. The conductor's success is not measured in volume, but in the coherence of performance.

Similarly, AI leaders do not write every line of code or design every dashboard. They create an environment where empowered teams can explore, align, and build together. The most impactful AI leaders act as orchestrators: aligning vision, building fluency, and nurturing a system that grows more capable over time.

The AI Leadership Playbook: 7 Moves That Matter

What does it take to be successful in your AI leadership journey? It starts by anchoring yourself around three critical levers: **Strategic Vision, Culture & Capability, and Delivery & Governance.** These levers represent the three domains every AI leader must influence:

- **Strategic Vision:** Defining purpose and aligning investments

- **Culture & Capability**: Developing people and empowering teams

- **Delivery & Governance:** Scaling responsibly and sustaining value

The leadership mindsets in this book are not standalone. They connect, complement, and reinforce the relationships between vision, capability, and governance.

Leadership change can be started with these simple 7 moves. Each of the 7 moves supports one or more of the levers.

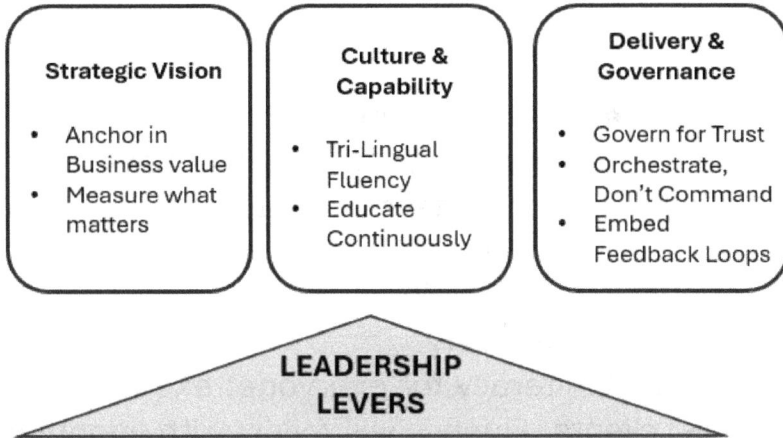

Strategic Vision	Culture & Capability	Delivery & Governance
• Anchor in Business value • Measure what matters	• Tri-Lingual Fluency • Educate Continuously	• Govern for Trust • Orchestrate, Don't Command • Embed Feedback Loops

LEADERSHIP LEVERS

1. Anchor in Business Value
- Connect AI conversations to strategic goals.
- Ask: How will this impact business outcomes?

2. Tri-Lingual Fluency
- Develop fluency in data, technology, and AI solutions.
- Communicate content, context, and enablers across teams.

3. Measure What Matters
- Redefine success metrics that connect AI solutions to outcomes across teams.
- Encourage cross-functional ownership of metrics.

4. Govern for Trust, Not Just Compliance
- Build governance at the enterprise level but promote Responsible AI at the team level.
- Encourage cross-team collaboration to build trust.

5. Orchestrate, Do not Command
- Empower teams to own actions and have flexibility to experiment with AI solutions.
- Lead through coordination and not control.

6. Educate Continuously
- Promote AI literacy for everyone: executives, users, clients. Fluency will follow with adoption.
- Champion role-based AI learning.

7. Embed Feedback Loops
- Treat every AI deployment as a prototype.
- AI is continuously learning, closely monitor its progress.

Intentional practice of these 7 basic moves will support the modern leaders to ensure that the organizational environment is better prepared to adopt and innovate with AI. Beyond three leadership levers, the 7 moves nurture the growth of AI fluency that bring organic innovators **from the edge into the mainstream organization.**

Your role as a leader is not to manage AI itself or be an expert but to **be an enabler**. AI leadership is most valued if you can ask the right questions, invite the right voices to the table, and steer the teams/organization with fluency, inclusivity, and intent.

The AI-Enabled Enterprise Is Always Evolving

The role of a leader is to create the right conditions for AI to thrive and add value at-scale. The most AI ready organizations are not those with the most models but those that are able to:
- Ask better questions
- Share learnings quickly
- Adapt faster to signals
- Build cultures that scale, not just the technologies

You do not need to have all the answers. But you must build systems that will adapt to your business.

Executive Reflection

1. What will it take for your organization to use AI as a strategy, not just a solution?
2. How are you shaping a culture where experimentation is safe and encouraged?
3. Are you applying AI to your toughest problems? Or just the easiest to automate?
4. Who owns AI literacy, measurement, and trust in your organization?

Call to Action: Pivot to an AI Leader

As you close this book, remember: AI success is not about knowing every answer, it is about asking better questions, nurturing the right environment, and leading with clarity and intention.

Start by identifying one initiative, one decision, or one team where your leadership can make AI more purposeful, more inclusive, and more aligned to your business goals. Use the table to initiate your first step towards this goal.

Summary

AI transformation is not about models: it is about mindset. It is about empowering people to explore new frontiers, supported by data, guided by purpose, and made resilient by feedback. Leadership is the glue that binds the parts of AI strategy together and brings it to life.

Lessons Learned

- Leadership determines how deeply AI is adopted, trusted, and scaled.
- Mindset shifts—toward orchestration, transparency, and value—are essential.
- The best AI organizations are learning organizations.
- Start with purpose. Lead with learning. And above all, design organizations—not just algorithms—that can learn and grow.

Getting Started: 90 Day Planner

Table 8: 90 Day Planner

Leadership Focus	Prompt	Your Reflection	Next Action Step
Purpose & Vision	What strategic outcome do I want AI to help achieve in the next 12 months?		
Leadership Behavior	Which of the 7 AI leadership moves am I actively modeling? Which one is missing?		
Team Engagement	Who in my organization needs to be more involved in shaping or scaling AI?		
Fluency Gaps	Where is our AI fluency weakest—data, technology, or decision alignment?		
Governance & Trust	Do we have clear structures for responsible AI use? Where are the risks today?		
Measurement & Impact	How are we defining and measuring AI success across business units?		
My Leadership Commitment	What's one mindset or practice I will change to better lead with AI?		

Resources

Figures and Tables

Glossary

AI – Artificial Intelligence
The field of computer science focused on building systems that simulate human intelligence. These systems can reason, learn, adapt, and perform tasks such as classification, prediction, and natural language understanding.

ML – Machine Learning
A subset of AI that enables computers to learn patterns from data and improve over time without being explicitly programmed. ML is the foundation for many predictive analytics and automation solutions.

GenAI – Generative AI
AI models capable of creating new content based on training data from: text, images, code, or audio. GenAI powers applications like chatbots, content generators, and code assistants.

GPT – Generative Pretrained Transformer
A type of large language model (LLM) trained on vast text datasets to generate human-like responses. GPT models, like ChatGPT, predict and compose text by analyzing context and intent.

HITL – Human-in-the-Loop
A system design approach where humans actively participate in the decision-making or feedback loop of

an AI process. HITL improves accuracy, trust, and accountability in AI systems.

AI Literacy
The basic awareness of how AI works, where it is used, and what its capabilities and limitations are. AI literacy is essential for non-technical users to engage meaningfully with AI tools.

AI Fluency
A step beyond literacy, AI fluency means understanding how to apply, interpret, and question AI in a business context. It requires cross-functional thinking across data, tech, and domain expertise.

Gemini, Claude, Bard, Anthropic, ChatGPT
Examples of GenAI platforms or tools developed by different companies:

- ChatGPT (OpenAI)
- Claude (Anthropic)
- Bard (Google, now integrated into Gemini)
- Gemini (Google's updated LLM platform)

These tools are designed for text generation, coding, summarization, and other language-based tasks.

Data Supply Chain
The lifecycle of how raw data is collected, transformed, governed, and delivered as usable input for AI systems. A healthy data supply chain ensures AI is fed reliable, timely, and business-aligned data.

Data Product

A use-case driven, reusable, self-contained and governed collection of curated data designed to solve specific business problem – Identity and Fraud Data Product.

AI Economic Value

The measurable business value generated from AI investments. It includes cost savings, revenue growth, productivity improvements, and risk reduction attributed to AI-enabled outcomes.

Tri-Lingual Fluency

The ability to speak the "three languages" of AI execution:

1. Technical (how the model works),
2. Data (where the inputs come from),
3. Domain (what the business impact is).
   Tri-lingual fluency enables alignment across teams.

Structured Data

Highly organized data that fits neatly into rows and columns—like databases or spreadsheets. It is commonly used in traditional ML models

Unstructured Data

Information that doesn't follow a strict format—such as images, documents, emails, and audio. GenAI systems are often designed to interpret unstructured data.

RADAR ©Wheel Data Strategies
A framework for responsible AI governance:

- **R**ead – Stay informed about your AI systems.
- **A**sk – Raise questions about fairness and impact.
- **D**ocument – Record decisions and data lineage.
- **A**cknowledge – Recognize risk or failure points.
- **R**eport – Escalate concerns and feedback responsibly.

AI Metrics
Model-specific performance indicators such as accuracy, precision, recall, F1 score, latency, and drift. These helps measure the technical effectiveness of AI systems.

Business Metrics
Outcome-oriented metrics like customer satisfaction, ROI, cost savings, revenue growth, or risk mitigation. These show whether AI delivers real business value.

Data Trust
The confidence users have in the accuracy, lineage, privacy, and integrity of the data powering AI systems. Trusted data is a prerequisite for scalable and responsible AI.

Responsible AI
The practice of designing, developing, and deploying AI systems that are ethical, transparent, fair, and

aligned with human values. It includes governance, risk management, and human oversight.

TaaS – Technology as a Service
It is defined here as the ability of the organization to establish a common modular technology platform for AI foundational services. This allows for easy curation of solutions, like a service, by the technology team instead of custom architecture for each business case.

Training-as-a-Service
AI is an evolving area where the nature of platforms, processes, solutions, and skills are constantly changing. Organizations should have the ability to create a process for delivering or seeking services that will continuously update, build AI fluency, along with technical AI literacy across the organization. This is not a one-time option.

ROI – Return on Investment
The Financial gain or loss generated from implementing AI technologies for an expected business outcome compared to the invested cost of building the foundations around *data, people, technology*, and *processes*.

Acknowledgments

The foundation for this book was laid in the moment the world discovered ChatGPT, with its pomp, circumstance, and provocative potential. I was captivated by its promise, but equally alert to the dissonance between the headlines and the hard realities of implementing AI inside organizations.

My own journey has been anything but linear. At times, stepping back from my career to "tick the right boxes" slowed my growth more than it nurtured it. I have learnt that real leadership, especially in AI, means staying sharp, curious, and deeply engaged. It means sharpening the saw continuously, not just admiring the tools.

Over the years, I have worked alongside thinkers, builders, visionaries, generalists, and yes procrastinators as well. From each, I have learned something. I owe special thanks to the communities that supported me: INFORMS, DAMA, TAG-Georgia, EDMC, WID, WIA, and ACM—for keeping the conversation honest, grounded, and stimulating.

A heartfelt thanks to Dr. Beverly Wright, a mentor, collaborator, and the one who first asked: Are we, as analytics leaders, truly preparing for what AI demands? Her influence sparked reflection, and eventually, a workshop, a newsletter (AI Unplugged), and this book.

I see tremendous opportunity in emerging technologies, but I also believe deeply in responsible and intentional use of them. Especially, when AI begins to influence business-critical or human-impacting decisions. The recent surge of fear, excitement, and misunderstanding about tools like ChatGPT, Bard, and Claude is not just a tech wave; it is a global social phenomenon.

That journey was amplified by conversations with peers on LinkedIn. What began as comment threads became real dialogue on how leaders think, where they struggle, and what helps them lead better.

I would be remiss not to thank my AI sidekick, Yoda (aka ChatGPT). For someone who never quite mastered Google search, Yoda helped me reach "search Nirvana", surfacing insights, prompts, and possibilities I had not considered. The new wave of GenAI tools truly democratized my learning journey and filled gaps in my awareness by accessing rich online information.

My deepest appreciation to the collaborators who shaped this book's spine: FinTech leaders, CAIOs, CDOs, CFOs, product strategists, and governance champions. They shared hard truths, bold ideas, and practical lessons. This book would not exist without feedback and hours of discussion around AI, data, and technology.

Collaborating with Dr. Colin Coleman on a data strategy workshop influenced the style of metaphor-based narration I adopted in this book. They help anchor abstract concepts in metaphors that resonate with real-world audiences.

To Sriram Tirunellayi, your insights on human-centric transformation and stakeholder alignment—drawn from our work supporting digital transformation with AI—deeply influenced my thinking on AI fluency roadmaps and governance models

To Neal Linson, Morgan Templar, and Shree Mukhopadhyay—thank you for grounding our conversations in the realities of practice and giving me the privilege of contributing to our collaborative work on defining the strategic value of data as an asset.

To Peter Maynard, for showing that AI leadership can be both deeply empathic and unapologetically rigorous. You demonstrated that a leader's true success is reflected in the growth and cohesion of their team. Thank you also for introducing me to Peter Luzmore's who framed 'The Synthesis Way'. A powerful blueprint for collaboration that continues to shape my approach.

To Anandhi, Alka, Raghu, and Faizan, your early reviews helped shape the tone, flow, and clarity of this book. Your time and thoughtful critique made the difference.

A callout to *Logos Ethos Pathos Publishing's* Stephen Templar in advising, editing, and supporting me on this writing journey through their services!

Finally, my husband, Badri Lokanathan, who has been my mirror, my challenger, and my partner in thoughts. Our dinner table has seen more architecture vs. economics showdowns than most conference rooms. This book owes its balance, and some of its best arguments, to those spirited negotiations over curry and code.

This book reflects not only what I have learned, but the shared wisdom of those I have had the privilege to learn from, stories of your experiences, suggestions, and honest hindsight of what could've gone differently.

Each of you has played a part in charting my course and been a guiding point in my **Leadership Compass**.

About the Author

Priya Sarathy is a passionate advocate for responsible AI, data strategy, and business transformation. With over 25 years of experience in analytics, enterprise data, and innovation leadership, she has guided organizations across industries from data chaos to insight-driven confidence.

As the founder of Wheel Data Strategies, Priya partners with small and mid-sized businesses navigating their first—and next—steps into the AI landscape. Her work blends strategic clarity with real-world execution, equipping business leaders to move beyond pilots and toward sustainable, scalable impact.

What sets Priya apart is her ability to simplify complexity. Whether guiding a CFO through AI investment decisions, helping a data team reframe their roadmap, or mentoring emerging leaders, she brings a unique mix of rigor, relevance, and empathy to every conversation.

She wrote AI Leadership Compass for the curious, the cautious, and the committed- leaders who want not just to use AI, but to lead with it. The book draws from the frameworks, case studies, and hard-won lessons she has shared in workshops, boardrooms, and classrooms alike. She is a frequent speaker at industry conferences and an invited guest at executive roundtables and ERG sessions.

Outside of work, Priya finds inspiration walking through city neighbourhoods, learning their history and exploring their parks and monuments. She volunteers with Trees Atlanta and several nonprofit professional groups. Her hobbies include tackling 5,000-piece puzzles as a form of focused meditation, and gardening—where selectively weeding out non-native plants becomes both a mental reset and a quiet study in the creativity of nature.

TO A SUCCESSFUL AI LEADERSHIP

References & Case Studies

Alaimo, Dan. 2018. "H&M turns to big data, AI to tailor store assortments." *RetailDive.* May. https://www.retaildive.com/news/hm-turns-to-big-data-ai-to-tailor-store assortments/523137/.

Alexander Hristov. 2023. *Wayfair's Mercury Feature Platform - FS Summit 23.* October. https://youtu.be/GCdyQ8ULlAE.

Alexis Wierenga. 2024. *Highlights From Gartner Data and Analytics Summit.* Mar. https://www.gartner.com/en/articles/highlights-from-gartner-data-analytics-summit-2024.

Andy Markus, Chief Data Officer, AT&T, interview by Founder & CEO, H2O.ai Sri Ambati. 2023. "H2O World: India ." *Fireside Chat with Andy Markus, AT&T & Sri Ambati, H2O.ai.* H2O. https://youtu.be/_QNxSR6zuIE.

AWS. 2022. *AWS Summit ATL 2022 - How Anthem uses AWS analytics to improve health outcomes (ADH201).* https://finance.yahoo.com/news/elevance-health-digital-transformation-strategy-140500809.html.

Bean, Randy. 2024. *Capital One: The Ongoing Story Of How One Firm Has Been Pioneering Data, Analytics, & AI Innovation For Over Three Decades.* Aug. https://www.forbes.com/sites/randybean/2024/08/11/capital-one-the-ongoing-story-of-how-one-firm-has-been-pioneering-data-analytics--ai-innovation-for-over-three-decades/.

Buolamwini, J. 2024. *Unmasking AI: My Mission to Protect What Is Human in a World of Machines.* Random House Publishing Group.

Chalmers, Brett. 2025. "AI for legal case strategy: Winning cases and clients." https://www.opus2.com/en-us/ai-for-legal-case-strategy/.

Chemitiganti, Vamsi. 2025. *Industry Spotlight – Engineering the AI Factory: Inside Netflix's AI Infrastructure.* May. https://www.vamsitalkstech.com/ai/industry-spotlight-engineering-the-ai-factory-inside-netflixs-ai-infrastructure-part-3/.

Covey, Stephen R. 2004. *https://www.goodreads.com/book/show/36072.The_7_Habits_of_Highly_Effective_People.* Free Press. https://www.goodreads.com/book/show/36072.The_7_Habits_of_Highly_Effective_People.

Dion, Martin. 2020. "Can AI be a force-multiplier for Intelligence Analysis?" *Research Gate.* doi:10.13140/RG.2.2.33630.05448.

Field, Hayden. 2024. "How Walmart, Delta, Chevron and Starbucks are using AI to monitor employee messages." *CNBC.* February. https://www.cnbc.com/2024/02/09/ai-might-be-reading-your-slack-teams-messages-using-tech-from-aware.html.

Floor Schuur, Mohammad H Rezazade Mehrizi, Erik Ranschaert. 2021. "Training opportunities of artificial intelligence (AI) in radiology: a systematic review." *Springer* Eur Radiol. 2021 Feb 15;31(8):6021–6029. doi: 10.1007/s00330-020-07621-y.

GRAB. 2024. "Kartacam 2 Mapping Award."
https://www.grab.com/sg/inside-grab/stories/kartacam-2-mapping-red-dot-design-award.

Grasso, Catie. 2025. *8 Steps to Drive AI Literacy Success.* Jan.
https://blog.dataiku.com/8-steps-to-drive-ai-literacy-success
.

Hari, Ravi. 2025. "Klarna's AI replaced 700 workers — Now the fintech CEO wants humans back after $40B fall." *Mint e-papers.* May.
https://www.livemint.com/companies/news/klarnas-ai-replaced-700-workers-now-the-fintech-ceo-wants-humans-back-after-40b-fall-11747573937564.html .

Hugging Face. 2022. *How Sempre Health is leveraging the Expert Acceleration Program to accelerate their ML roadmap.* May. https://huggingface.co/blog/sempre-health-eap-case-study.

IBIS World. 2025. *Driving Schools in the US - Market Research Report (2015-2030.* June.
https://www.ibisworld.com/united-states/industry/driving-schools/4995/ .

IBM . 2025. "Case Studies."
https://www.ibm.com/products/maximo/case-studies.

IBM Technology. 2023. *Apollo.io.* Aug. https://youtu.be/T-D1OfcDW1M?si=NsMCju3JA2PjRfO8 .

Infra.com. 2025. "Amazon's robotics revolution: How AI is transforming warehouse operations." *Infra.com,* March. https://infra.economictimes.indiatimes.com/news/logistics/a

mazons-robotics-revolution-how-ai-is-transforming-
warehouse-operations/118883206.

Kelly, Megan. 2024. "How GM is boosting resiliency through
predictive AI tools." *Automotive Logistics.*
https://wwww.automotivelogistics.media/digital-
technology/how-gm-is-boosting-resiliency-through-
predictive-ai-tools/46133.article.

Lufthansa Systems. 2024. *Neos chooses Lufthansa Systems for crew
management of growing fleet.* Aug.
https://cloud.google.com/blog/topics/sustainability/lufthansa
-uses-data-to-reduce-carbon-emissions-of-airline-travel.

Marr, Bernard. 2018. "How Fashion Retailer H&M Is Betting On
Artificial Intelligence And Big Data To Regain
Profitability." *Forbes.* Jan.
https://www.forbes.com/sites/bernardmarr/2018/08/10/how-
fashion-retailer-hm-is-betting-on-artificial-intelligence-and-
big-data-to-regain-profitability.

McKinsey Blog. 2025. "An inside look at how McKinsey helped
DBS become an AI-powered bank." *McKinsey & Company.*
Feb. https://www.mckinsey.com/about-us/new-at-mckinsey-
blog/an-inside-look-at-how-mckinsey-helped-dbs-become-
an-ai-powered-bank?utm_source=chatgpt.com.

Microsoft. 2023. *Microsoft Build Conference 2023 .* Mar.
https://www.youtube.com/watch?v=FaV0tIaWWEg.

—. 2025. *2025 Responsible AI Transparency Report: How we
build, support our customers, and grow.* May. https://cdn-
dynmedia-
1.microsoft.com/is/content/microsoftcorp/microsoft/msc/do

cuments/presentations/CSR/2025-Responsible-AI-Transparency-Report.pdf.

Neumeister, Larry. 2025. *An AI avatar tried to argue a case before a New York court. The judges weren't having it.* AP News.com. https://apnews.com/article/artificial-intelligence-ai-courts-nyc-5c97cba3f3757d9ab3c2e5840127f765 .

NIST. 2023. "Artificial Intelligence Risk Management Framework (AI RMF 1.0)." National Institute of Standards and Technology. https://www.nist.gov/itl/ai-risk-management-framework.

OpenAI. 2025. *Morgan Stanley uses AI evals to shape the future of financial services.* https://openai.com/customer-stories/morgan-stanley.

Patel, Bhushan Jayeshkumar. 2024. "AI-Powered Robotic Surgery: Pushing The Boundaries Of Minimally Invasive Procedures." *Forbes.* October. https://www.forbes.com/councils/forbestechcouncil/2024/10/29/ai-powered-robotic-surgery-pushing-the-boundaries-of-minimally-invasive-procedures/.

Pfizer. 2022. *Accelerating Digital Technology for the COVID-19 Vaccine Rollout.* Mar. https://www.pfizer.com/news/behind-the-science/accelerating-digital-technology-covid-19-vaccine-rollout.

Pindrop. 2024. *86-Year-Old Credit Union Cuts Authentication Time in Half in First 90 Days of Pindrop Implementation.* Pindrop, Case Study. https://www.pindrop.com/research/case-study/michigan-state-university-federal-credit-union/.

Pinterest. 2023. *Pinterest announces industry-first body type technology to increase body representation on platform.* September. https://newsroom.pinterest.com/news/pinterest-announces-industry-first-body-type-technology/.

Praveen Ravichandran, Marco De Nadai, Divita Vohra, Sandeep Ghael, Manizeh Khan, Paul Bennett, Tony Jebara, Mounia Lalmas-Roelleke. 2024. *R&D.* Dec. https://research.atspotify.com/2024/12/contextualized-recommendations-through-personalized-narratives-using-llms/.

Priya Sarathy, Wheel Data Strategies. 2024. "Data-Driven Dynamics: Transforming Financial Services Through Analytics." *INFORMS Business Analytics Conference.* Orlando.

SAP. 2025. "MOD Pizza: Breaking down barriers to equitable job opportunities with connected HR." *SAP Customer Stories.* https://www.sap.com/asset/dynamic/2023/07/623a5dca-807e-0010-bca6-c68f7e60039b.html.

Sarathy, Priya. 2024. *Navigating the Ethical Minefield: Professional Responsibility in Unknown Territory of AI Deployment.* September. https://www.wheelds.com/post/navigating-the-ethical-minefield-professional-responsibility-in-unknown-territory-of-ai-deployment.

Stitch Fix . 2025. *MultiThreaded: Algorithms Tour- How data science is woven into the fabric of Stitch FIx.* https://algorithms-tour.stitchfix.com/.

Stroh, Kelly. 2024. "GM increases supply chain visibility with Optilogic." *SUPPLYCHAINDIVE.*

https://www.supplychaindive.com/news/general-motors-supply-chain-visibility-optilogic-sku/720444/.

Synapse. 2025. "5 Emerging Fraud Patterns in Digital Lending & How AI Stops Them." Synapse Analytics. https://synapse-analytics.io/blog/5-emerging-fraud-patterns-in-digital-lending-how-ai-stops-them.

Unilever. 2025. *How AI is transforming Unilever Ice Cream's end-to-end supply chain.* Jan. https://www.unilever.com/news/news-search/2025/how-ai-is-transforming-unilever-ice-creams-end-to-end-supply-chain/.

Virti. 2022. "Scaling simulation training and reducing in-person training by 50%." *Virti Customer Stories.* https://www.virti.com/customer-stories/cedars-sinai/.

Wikipedia. 2025. *2021 Texas power crisis.* https://en.wikipedia.org/wiki/2021_Texas_power_crisis .

Wilkinson, M. D., Dumontier, M., Aalbersberg, I. J., et al. 2016. "The FAIR Guiding Principles for scientific data management and stewardship. Scientific Data, ." *Scientific Data.*

Wilson, Linda. 2023. "John Deere Uses Machine Vision and Machine Learning to Automate Agriculture." *Vision Systems Design.* May. https://www.vision-systems.com/non-factory/environment-agriculture/article/14293351/john-deere-uses-machine-vision-and-machine-learning-to-automate-agriculture.

Zoom Blog. 2024. *Meet Zoom AI Companion, your new AI assistant! Unlock the benefits with a paid Zoom account.* July. https://blog.zoom.us/zoom-ai-companion/.

www.ingramcontent.com/pod-product-compliance
Lightning Source LLC
Chambersburg PA
CBHW070927210326
41520CB00021B/6833